C000244505

Praise for

"An absolute outrage and totally insulting, this book makes the French out to be lazy and incompetent; it also implies that Waterloo was a defeat for the French army"...

Mayor of the village of Loser

"Every time I read a book about mayhem and a general lack of any work ethic it seems to include Stanley George. I can only conclude that he is the common denominator".....

Editor of Please Wipe Your Boots

"This means war!"....

The President

Also by Stanley George

Please Wipe Your Boots

The crazy mayhem that once was your telephone
exchange finally exposed.

FRENCH FARCE

A journey into mayhem

By

STANLEY GEORGE

Contents

"How can you govern a country that has 246 different varieties of cheese?"

Charles de Gaulle

FOREWORD

Now here's a thing; can you remember that feeling when you shut the front door, climbed into your car and drove off on holiday? Great feeling wasn't it?

But what if you were not coming back? What if there was nothing to come back to? Well, that's where we were 13 years ago.

House sold, caravan bought, car filled with fuel, channel tunnel crossing booked, dogs injected with a large variety of drugs and there we sat.....with nowhere to go.

We had no specific place in mind other than 'somewhere in France'. After many enjoyable French holidays, we had long discussed the possibility of actually living there; and early retirement had given us both the reason and opportunity.

This is a story of those early years in France and in particular tells a tale of the strange and sometimes bizarre people that are....the French. There are many books written on living in France but the difference here is an in-depth humorous analysis of the 'laissez faire' attitude of French village folk. You will experience their sometimes infuriating, sometimes crazy view of life; and experience the basic mayhem that makes up their normal day to day existence.

To be fair to those individuals I have changed some place names and the names of most of the participants. After all, I still live in France and the guillotine was still legal up to 1981, thus hasn't gone rusty yet! Also, I have condensed some of the timings to make for a better flow.

Hopefully along the way I will be able to educate as well as amuse as I pick out some of the pitfalls of living here in France. I will also introduce some historical insights that may change your view of how things were.

As an additional bonus you will be treated to a breakdown of how to swear in French, which is a must for anyone travelling in Europe. Those easily offended may wish to skip over this part!

Now let's be clear, this is not intended to be a rant against all things French. This book will highlight the odd behaviour and culture change shock when initially confronted with actually living in France. This is an experience that cannot be gained from holidays alone.

So, sit back and follow our route through mayhem and ponder this, would you, could you take the risk?

CHAPTER ONE

Arrivals and Introductions

The village of Loser *(carefully pronounced Loo-say)* nestles quietly in the Midi Pyrenees minding its own business as it has done for centuries. With about 120 inhabitants it represents about 20% of what was once a village full of shops, schools and bustle.

Like most small French villages there is a contraction of the population as shops close and young people move out to the bigger towns for employment. Leaving behind empty stone houses, many ancient folks, an impressive very large 'Mairie' *(Townhall)* and quiet....very, very quiet.

How we ended up in this location is still a puzzle. Basically for us the Midi Pyrenees was an area yet unexplored, thus seemed an ideal first port of call to get a feel for the possibilities of a permanent home. By sheer chance an ancient stone farmhouse was up for sale when we arrived, and after checking out alternatives we were hooked.

The French call it 'coup de coeur' or as we would say, let your heart rule your head!

So, there we were, house bought, caravan parked, car out of fuel, dogs with even more drugs and now sat on the terrace of an old farmhouse recently renovated to a 'very high' standard. All this with the rear of the furniture removal lorry slowly disappearing through the gates.

Let's just expand on this just a bit. Car out of fuel because at that time everything, even supermarkets, were shut for a long lunch. Only a few garages then had 24/7 fuel pumps and even these would only accept a French credit card! Thus, if you were low on fuel coming up to lunchtime you were screwed.

Even worse, if you were low on fuel on Sunday you were not going anywhere till Monday. We will expand more on this lunchtime, daytime or anytime closure of anything commercial a bit later.

Dogs with even more drugs; because it would appear that this part of France, due to sheep farming, is endemic with ticks including ones that can kill. We decided not to mention this to the dogs. And when I say kill, I do not mean just dogs!

Renovated to a high standard? Well firstly those who were hoping for a blow by blow account of how to buy a property in France will be disappointed. I will leave that to the hundreds of other books that cover the subject. Suffice it to say that it was a long, costly, and a bureaucratic nightmare that tests both your nerves and your wallet. As to renovation, what looked like a good job was slowly revealed to be....not a good job.

Our first taste of this challenge to 'Estate Agent speak' being the first thunderstorm; day three I think. Where, as well as rain cascading down the outside of the house, a good deal was also cascading down the inside. The first of many wallet bashing changes to that renovation.

The seller of the house, a Brit I might add, seemed to have a reputation learned later of 'doing up' property on the cheap, selling and quickly moving on. He also did everything himself; badly.

So, your first French lesson, only buy a property that has guarantees for any completed work from an artisan. These guarantees cover you for mishaps for 10 years, but the downside is the inflated prices that French artisans charge for their work.

Actually, becoming an artisan in France seemed to be quite difficult with numerous examinations and the usual bureaucracy. A Dutch plumber who lived nearby in the Lot Department went to the 'Préfecture' *(the centre for administration)* with all his extensive Dutch plumbing qualification to claim his artisan status.

On producing his documents and asking for his French artisan recognition he was simply told no; he would have to take all the French exams.

"But all these qualifications that I have are European," he explained.

"This is not Europe, this is the Lot!" came the staggering response.

So back to our own situation, there we were sat in a bit of a daze, the proud owners of an old farmhouse in the middle of nowhere. We were surrounded by our UK possessions which unfortunately overflowed into a covered terrace at the back of the house. At this critical moment came our first meeting with one of the new French 'voisins' *(neighbours)*.

First came the smell, then came the rustle of movement of a large number of animals. This slowly grew louder until up the small road by the side of our house a dust covered flock of sheep came into view. A motlier flock of sheep I have never seen.

Most seemed to have something wrong with them, either limping or hopping along the road. They were very dirty and smelled, boy did they smell. Behind them casually strolled Jean-Pierre dragging behind him a collie dog tied to a rope; the local shepherd.

Our own dogs were very excited about this sudden development and ran excitedly up and down the inside of the garden wall as the sheep and Jean-Pierre ambled by. This they persisted in doing every time the sheep went by for many, many years. The sheep never once even turned to see what was making the fuss.

It's hard to describe the impact of a first sighting of this character but perhaps it is best achieved by describing his appearance and let you picture it in your mind. And remember it, as you will be bumping into Jean-Pierre at regular intervals throughout the book.

Slight of build at around 68 years of age, skin looking like tanned leather. Dressed in aging clothes that all looked like they had once belonged either to his dad or granddad. Battered, stained trousers held up by a piece of blue string covering an equally battered pair of boots.

A shirt that once was white, then grey, now beige covered by an equally battered cardigan....similar colour. And an aging jacket that once belonged perhaps to a suit, someone else's suit...a long time ago. All this was topped off by a battered cap worn at a jaunty angle.

The jacket by the way was a permanent feature. Whatever the weather be it hot, wet, cold, snow, sleet or typhoon he would be seen ambling along in his jacket. The only concession he made to bitter cold was a change of cap to woolly hat....with a bobble on the top.

He also made a vital fashion statement by actually buttoning up the jacket whilst riding along on his aging moped. This concession was also evident whilst he was out hunting in minus 20 degrees!

If your imagination is struggling with all this try 'googling' Worzel Gummidge and you have a close enough picture.

Being dragged reluctantly behind Jean-Pierre came an aging collie dog that looked like he would rather be somewhere else, anywhere else.

Now here's a thing, I always thought that collie dogs herded sheep, kept them together, moved them to where you wanted them to go but no, this one seemed to be redundant. It had no purpose other than to slow Jean-Pierre down as he dragged him along.

In a country where nearly all dogs seemed to roam the streets off lead causing chaos and crapping wherever they liked, this dog was the exception. Perhaps the only time it was critical for a dog to be off lead on the road, he was firmly on one. And he stayed on one throughout the day and throughout all his sorry life.

So, here was my chance; my chance to introduce myself and test the extensive French vocabulary learned from my school days at Brooke House Comprehensive. The alumni included Lord Alan Sugar so that should give you a good indication of the sort of rubbish school it was.

To be fair, the French teacher Mr Jackson was probably quite good as during the war he had something to do with the French resistance, or so he said. All I remember clearly is the incredible smell of garlic that emanated from his classroom and his insistence that everyone stand and say something in French at each lesson.

My offering was 'Il fait beau' *(nice weather we are having)* for years....and years. The first couple of years I didn't even bother to learn what this meant. And Mr Jackson had long given up on teaching anything to a group of scallywags. It was clear to him that their only interest was rolling the next cigarette behind the cycle racks. So, he let this ride.

But I was not going to let this opportunity slip by, so I bounded down the farmhouse stairs to stand by the gate as Jean-Pierre sauntered by.

"Bonjour, il fait beau," I said.

"Grrrahe mer merggrr gru grunbbrr," he replied, while looking me up and down as if I had just beamed down from the Starship Enterprize.

"Er! I er! ...il fait beau?" I repeated, desperately looking over my shoulder for an escape route from this embarrassment.

"GR GRRAHE MER MERGGRR G GRU," he answered, obviously intending that his increased sound level made it easier for me to understand.

So, picture the scene, here I was having a conversation with a tramp in a foreign country who stuttered, didn't speak any language known to man and smelled rather strongly of sheep. So, I nodded, he nodded and off he strolled. The collie leaving his own calling card on the floor by the gate!

He passed back again at lunchtime, sheep and dog in tow. He passed by again after lunch or 3 hours later whichever is longest, sheep and dog in tow and returned in the evening sheep and dog in tow.

This process repeated itself every day and was baffling; why didn't he just leave the sheep in his fields all the time. This current modus operandi necessitated a 2km walk both there and back twice a day in sun, rain, hail, wind and snow.

It didn't make sense so a few weeks later, through an interpreter, I asked him.

"Why don't you just leave the sheep out in the field and bring them back just when you need to?" I enquired.

"Because it's always been done like that," he responded.

And that was that, it had always been done like that, end of. No question of moving on, developing new modus operandi, or even tweaking the procedure a little bit. If it was good enough for his great, great grandfather it was good enough for him.

The same response was given to my stunning revelation that collie dogs can be left to herd the sheep in any direction he wanted. A slow shake of the head demonstrated that he thought I was joking; this conversation was going nowhere.

It is interesting to note that after many months of French lessons *(Mr Jackson would be laughing his head off)* I discussed my inability to understand Jean-Pierre with a Parisian who worked in the village.

He laughed and explained that nobody understood Jean-Pierre as he spoke his own family version of regional 'patois'. *(A regional language variant that was mostly only spoken.)* This was unfortunately mixed with a bit of Spanish topped off with some French all rounded off by a stutter!

Worryingly after many years living in the village I actually started to understand him!

That first afternoon, whilst trying to find items buried inside innumerable cardboard boxes, I spotted a second 'voisin'. This time standing in the road at the rear of our house staring at the pile of overflow removal boxes.

This strange lady seemed transfixed by our belongings and her 1,000-yard stare was a bit unsettling. On seeing me, she shuffled off back to Jean-Pierre's farm glancing back over her shoulder on several occasions.

She was in fact Jean-Pierre's wife, a more bizarre pair you will never meet. Her name was Madeline with emphasis on the first syllable.

She was dressed in a similar outfit to Jean-Pierre without the jacket but attired in an oversized woolly jumper.

She was without doubt much younger than Jean-Pierre and had the most amazing hair style. Basically, it looked as though she had been electrocuted with all her hair stuck in an upright position.

I became intrigued to know how these two came together and at a village function asked a local guy if he knew. He did, and explained the whole story. At some time previously Jean-Pierre's mother decided that he needed a wife, and discussed this requirement with the family of a friend who lived in a village nearby.

Apparently in the family were three unmarried sisters, who whilst, how can I put this, not being of the highest IQ were ready, willing and able to take on marriage.

Jean-Pierre was introduced to the sisters and came straight to the point.

"Can any of you drive a tractor?" he gallantly enquired.

"Me," said Madeline whilst putting up her hand to emphasise the point.

"You'll do," he responded in true gentlemanly fashion.

And that was that, they got married. And it must have been love because, like a gentleman, he would sometimes let her walk the sheep whenever he had a bit of fun tractor driving to do.

I, of course, laughed at this proposal story assuming it to be a joke. However, its accuracy was much later confirmed by Jean-Pierre himself adding that this was not unusual in the tiny countryside villages in France. Well, I have heard of arranged marriages before of course, but never one where the ability to drive a tractor was the main criteria.

We will meet Jean-Pierre many times in this book as his chaotic antics are worthy of note. And I will state here and now that he was one of the kindest, most helpful guys I have ever met. Always willing to help with any issue, a font of knowledge about the people who lived in Loser and best of all had that seldom seen ability to laugh at himself whenever things got daft...really daft.

It's worth perhaps introducing some other characters who made life in the village so entertaining. Firstly Henri, pronounced locally Onree, and his wife Brigette. Our farmhouse overlooked their cottage, but I quickly discovered that their cottage overlooked our farmhouse as Brigette seemed to always know what we were doing...all the time.

Once at an 'apero' *(aperitif or drinks as we would say)* someone asked me what time I had to get up for the dogs in the morning. "About 6.30," said Brigette before I had a chance to say anything!

This actually had a plus side as we always left our home on holiday safe in the knowledge that nobody could possibly approach our farmhouse. They would be carefully appraised by Brigette, and woe betide anyone who should not have been there; she took no prisoners.

Henri was in his seventies but was incredibly fit and seemed always to be doing something, be it logging or maybe rebuilding stones walls. Always dressed smartly in a country jacket, moving slowly with hands clasped behind his back, he just got on with stuff all the time.

He was the proud owner of one of the largest log piles I have ever seen. It filled a huge purpose made barn, and I mean huge. This log collection continued under cover around most of his extensive field.

Now French guys have a thing about log stacks; there seems to be a competition as to who can have the biggest. Well no one was getting anywhere near the size of Henri's stack; yet he continued to cut down more and more trees. Therefore he continued to pile up more and more logs.

I'm sure Sigmund Freud could have explained it all, but all I know is that I wasn't playing this game. I sadly stacked only one year's worth of logs at a time, which I cleverly paid someone else to chop up.

I did attempt this logging challenge just once. A local friend, 'The Professor' who we will meet later, offered 'free of charge' trees to be cut down on a piece of land he had bought for hunting. I contacted a good friend of mine from the UK, Eric, and proposed a fun week of chopping down trees and cutting them up into logs ready for stacking.

It must have been a great sales job as he was keen and accepted this challenge....what could possibly go wrong?

Well everything really. There should be some law against folk walking into a shop and buying a chainsaw, and then being let loose in the countryside chopping down trees! It was dangerous to say the least, very time consuming, incredibly hard work and for a whole week of back breaking effort I still didn't seem to have enough logs for a full winters fuel.

This is not forgetting the near miss decapitations, close shave broken limbs and moments of sheer terror as the trees fell in the wrong direction...by that I mean our direction. And after all that, the logs would need drying out before splitting into a usable size; never again. After that week whatever price I saw for cut and split, fire-ready logs looked cheap!

Stacking logs is also hard work but I came up with the perfect solution to this problem. In his book The Adventures of Tom Sawyer, Mark Twain explains that burdened by the chore of whitewashing his aunt Polly's fence as a punishment; Tom comes up with an ingenious way to get out of this work.

He convinces his friends that that is not tedious hard labour at all but rather something enjoyable. In fact, it's an artform, a skill with results to be proud of. Thus, one after the other his friends happily whitewash the wall for him. Well sorry Eric and Ken now you have read this you know you were had. Still, better than going to the gym wasn't it?

Now Henri, much like Jean-Pierre, presented me with a communications challenge. That is to say, I couldn't understand a word he said. Even after many French lessons his guttural responses left me puzzled. One thing I did not anticipate before arriving was the problem of isolated rural French villages and their language history.

Firstly, the accent was strong, very strong; very much like asking for directions in Glasgow only to get the response in Glaswegian. Secondly, some parts of France were once not France. And various regions had their own languages which flourished.

People spoke Alsatian, Catalan, Basque, Corsican, Breton, Gallo Occitan and so on. In fact, I am reliably informed that written Occitan predates written French. And at the time of the French revolution in 1789 only half the population of France could actually speak French!

Once France became a unified country, regional languages were pretty much banned. And only French was taught at school; but the various types of patois lived on in family homes particularly in the smaller villages.

However, in April 2001 the Minister of Education for France admitted formally that for more than two centuries the political powers of the French government had repressed regional languages. He then announced that bilingual education would, for the first time, be recognised and bilingual teachers recruited in French schools.

In 2008 a revision to the French constitution created official recognition of these regional languages. This change of heart has seen their resurgence with youngsters being taught them at school, thus they live on. A great example of this is the 5-year-old grandson of a local friend. He could switch between French to English to Occitan without a thought.

So back to Henri and his deeply accented mixture of patois and French. I was fascinated by the somewhat overprovisioned log storage scenario and I decided to ask him, with much hand gesturing, how old the lower logs in the barn were.

"My grandfather started them," he said. So basically, what I was looking at was a stack of logs started some time before the First World War!

Another of Henri's passions was his garden which included vast amounts of vegetables, fruit trees, dozens of chickens and a huge warren of rabbits. The downside of this became apparent when about 200 lettuces were ready at the same time.

Each day he trotted over to our house with a box of lettuces, each time we thanked him and not feeling able to say no took them in. Then it was cherries, then it was strawberries and so on.

During this period various other village folks would stop in their cars and ask if we wanted any lettuces. My enquiry as to where they were all coming from was universally met by "Henri keeps giving them to us!"

The final straw came when he asked if I could give him a hand catching some of his rabbits. Naively I said "of course." I followed him to the rabbit warren in his huge garden, and there followed a strange procedure of blocking and opening various entrances to the warren. All this time while either covering or opening the partitioned roofing.

Whilst baffling to me, Henri seemed to know exactly what he was doing, and we eventually ended up with one particular part of the warren being full of rabbits.

There now followed the cull. Those of a delicate disposition need to look away now. One after another he selected the plumpest looking rabbits, grabbed them by the ears, dispatched them quickly with a thump to the back of the neck and piled them up.

His intention of course was a freezer refill. When he decided that he had enough he would simply open up all the warren entrances and partitions again, and life would go on for the remaining rabbits. I thought he was finished and was somewhat relieved when he indicated an end to the proceedings.

As a final gesture he picked up two cute looking bunnies and asked me what I thought of them. "Very nice," I said, meaning cute....WHACK!... "Here you are then, thanks for the help," he said. I wandered slowly back to our house somewhat shell shocked holding up a dead rabbit in each hand. My wife was not amused.

All of this led to me organising my own small vegetable patch at the rear of the house. Not to really grow vegetables of course, merely to give me an excuse not to need any of Henri's overproduced offerings. He often strolled by and looked, sadly shaking his head, at the pathetic produce that limply existed on my patch.

Next to his production line it must have been a puzzle to Henri as to why I even bothered. What made it worse was the fact that my vegetable patch was next to my size challenged log stack; thus producing even more shaking of the head as he wandered by.

One thing that I did not copy from Henri was the repeated attacks on various wildlife that had the temerity to land on his produce. Every so often a very loud bang from a shotgun was followed by an equally loud French curse from Henri as another bird nibbled at his cherry tree. This was occasionally followed by a loud shout of "FANNY," as he called his hunting dog out as backup.

It seemed as though he spent most of the day looking out across his garden just waiting for a bird to land. And Fanny definitely had plenty of exercise. I tried to explain to him the reason why I found his shouting of Fanny, at the top of his voice, so funny. But without much luck, he just didn't see it.

A few years later, as Fanny was getting on in years, he turned up one day with a new puppy. Unbelievably, the new puppy's name was Dick!

The next candidate for introduction is in fact another 'voisin'. This time the 'Maire' *(Mayor)* of Loser himself, a Monsieur Francois Sangbon. Now you could argue that the role of Mayor in France is an important job. After all they get to say yes or no to most village activities and are the first port of call for all village problems.

And indeed, I am sure that the Mayor of Paris is a very important job but Loser.....with about 120 people? And with about 36,500 Mayors in France you have to wonder how far down the list Loser appears.

I must admit though the 'Mairie' was very impressive, it was huge and emblazoned with a very large MAIRIE sign that left no doubt as to its importance. However, the sad fact was that only a small office on the ground floor was actually used for this official role.

You will see this mirrored throughout France. When you want to know where the Mairie is in any small village just look for the biggest, most impressive building you can find.

However, for Francois Sangbon it was the most important job in the world. As an ex-military man, Lieutenant Colonel no less, he approached the role of village Mayor with the precision expected from a military campaign. Every 'I' dotted, every 'T' crossed, all ducks neatly lined up in a row and everyone doing as they are told.

That is, until we turned up. The first thing we noticed about our Mayor was that he ignored us. Every day he drove past our house on his way to the Mairie. Every time we waved and shouted 'bonjour', and every time he glanced the other way and blanked us.

So, we decided not just to wave but stand and wave both hands enthusiastically shouting 'bonjour' at the top of our voices. Finally we achieved a breakthrough; he turned and nodded.

Now don't get me wrong here, he turned out to be a very helpful friend but to put you into the picture of what he was really like I quote two examples. Firstly, whenever we gave him some cash from the village bar *(more about this venture later)* he would not accept it until he had turned every note the right way up and facing the same way.

You could see a bead of perspiration on his forehead until he had accomplished this totally unnecessary task. Secondly, whenever we attended a local Loto *(again, bear with me, I will cover this later)* he made a note of every number that was called and its sequence.

Yes, you did just read that; every single number called! Now, I don't want to keep bringing Sigmund Freud back into this French Farce but I'm sure he would have loved to watch Francois for hours.

However, there are certainly some personality traits that you can turn to your advantage. If we needed any information, we didn't do any research we just asked the Mayor, this in the absolute certainty that he would do the unending research and provide the correct answer.

Any paperwork that needed signing just ask the Mayor. His chest would puff out, his useful existence as Mayor was confirmed and the paperwork would be completed to perfection.

Knowing what he was like I cleverly mentioned that I would quite like to join the local chasse.

(The classic French hunting fraternity. I will devote a whole chapter to this exclusive club, and whatever your thoughts on hunting you will find it fascinating)

He immediately took me under his wing as a 'Chasser Accompagné' *(basically his apprentice)* and paraded me up and down the hunting fields for 4 months continually bleating on about how he scored 21/21 in his chasse exam.

He did have one embarrassing moment though. In order to practice with an over & under style of shotgun *(necessary for the practical section of the chasse examinations)* I asked to borrow his. No problem, and he accordingly obliged.

On further inspection of the aforementioned 'fusil' *(shotgun)* I immediately noticed the rather disgusting state of the inside of the barrel.

33

"Er! When was the last time you actually cleaned this gun?" I asked

"Not for a while," he responded, while looking somewhat sheepish.

"Aren't you supposed to clean these after each use?" I said, clearly now backing him into an awkward corner.

"Technically yes, but I haven't used it for a while," he waffled.

"So, an ex-Lieutenant Colonel in the French army hands me a weapon with a dirty barrel!

What would be the punishment for that in the army?" I casually enquired.

"I'm not in the army now and anyway I won't tell if you don't," he replied.

And for the first time since we had met, he burst into laughter.

These walks during my hunting apprenticeship helped greatly with my learning of the French language as he was forced to talk about something. He had no paperwork to sign, no paper money to line up and no one to impress. Plus, he had quickly worked out that I really didn't care what his previous career had been.

34

This was probably exacerbated by me whistling 'Hail to the Chief' the USA Presidential anthem whenever he walked into a room. Nobody else noticed, but he did!

(Actually, he was wrong about not being impressed; on a visit once to his house I noticed a very nice medal in a case on the wall. On asking what it was, he explained that it was his 'Légion d'Honneur', the highest French order of merit for both military and civil achievements. And I can tell you this, they are not handed out like sweeties! Very impressive.)

It was during these chats that we had our first disagreement; and by chance it was based on military history. I just happen to mention that the French army had been soundly beaten by the Brits on many occasions. His astounding response was that this had never happened at all.

So, ignoring 1066 because that was nothing to do with France, I dived in.

(They were Normans who were all basically descended from Vikings; thus it was the normal Viking-Saxon dispute. That is if you forget the Bretons and Flemish who were lending William a hand.)

"What about Agincourt then?" I commenced.

"Merely a battle cut short by very poor weather conditions and poor choice of kit," he responded.

"Okay then, what about Crécy?" I countered.

"Doesn't count as the English unsportingly used cannons," he replied.

"And Trafalgar?" I continued, now running out of actual battles.

"Simply a cock up by the Spanish," he said.

And now for my 'Coup de Grâce.'

"Okay, what about Waterloo then, you cannot deny that was a defeat?" I proudly challenged.

"Outrageous." he said. "That was an expertly performed military retreat from the Prussians!"

At this stage I had to give up as I had exhausted my pool of famous French defeats and he seemed to have a good answer for all of them. I could have mentioned the fact that the French National flag between 1814 and 1830 was plain white *(oh yes it was, look it up)* which seemed to follow these 'defeats'; but I really do not think his sense of humour would have stretched that far.

Strangely I did mention Waterloo on several occasions to a variety of other French folks and none of them considered it a defeat. So, who is kidding who I wonder!

There are many other characters to meet in the book, but I think we will let their stories unfold as we go along. From guys who could only say one sentence in English, to an aging Lothario with the biggest garage in the world, from an ex RAF rear gunner, to an aging lady who thought I was the Gestapo, and from feuding families to the 'Professor' of pétanque. You will meet them all along the way.

CHAPTER TWO

Christmas Offerings & the Crèche

As it was nearing Christmas we decided that it was time to introduce ourselves formally to these new neighbours. We therefore planned an informal 'drinks and mince pie' evening at the farmhouse. Now bear in mind that, at this stage, our knowledge of the French language was somewhat limited; if you remember for me it was 'Il fait beau' and luckily for my wife it was a few words more.

Also remember that the neighbours, for the most part, could not speak a word of English and were even questionable on actually speaking French. So, this was going to be a fun evening.

We ended up inviting a large number of surrounding villagers expecting only a small number to turn up. They all turned up. And our pathetic knowledge of French was tested to destruction and beyond. Now here's a thing, if you thought we were nervous about inviting the French into our home; think about them. They had never been invited into a Brit's home before, even though there were several other British folks in the village.

Therefore, they had spent several days of panicked phone calls between themselves, other villages, various Mayors, anyone who could speak a word of English and anyone who had ever in their life been to the UK.

This with one question in mind, what do the British expect from their guests when invited over for a drink? They also had spent days of deep internet analysis on what actually constitutes a 'mince pie'.

But slowly they turned up, each bearing suitable gifts of flowers or even a bottle of Champagne. The fact that no gift was duplicated bears witness to the amount of preparation they had undertaken just to pop round for a drink!

I also noticed that flowers had to be odd in number as even numbered flowers as a gift is unlucky in France. Says a lot about the traditional dozen roses given in the UK!

First to turn up was the Mayor and his wife, and after 'bonjour' and the very British discussion of the weather *(here you quickly learn that for cold they say, "not hot" and for hot they say, "not cold" etc.)* we just stood looking at each other. We had depleted our French and they only knew the English words 'mince pie' which they had googled before arrival.

As it transpired, they were expecting a minced beef pie and were rather disappointed with the fruity offering on the table. We explained mince pies by simply saying it was a traditional British dish; this they readily accepted.

So much so in fact that whenever we invited folk over for food in the future, and the actual cooking process had resulted in a bit of a mess; we simply said that this was the traditional British way of cooking it and everyone was happy!

After the mayor came Bernard, the local plumber. Now, by plumber I actually mean plumber, roofer, builder, chimney sweep or anything that you actually want doing but do not want to pay the exorbitant artisan prices for. In his early fifties he always seemed somewhat worse for wear with drink or at least smelled of the stuff.

He also habitually had a cigarette dangling from his mouth. *(Years later, due to bad health, he stopped drinking and looked ten years younger.)*

I thought his very casual attire was very fitting for a builder until I learned that this was his normal dress choice on every occasion. We used him several times for work on the farmhouse and each time he never let us down.

The pipework may have not been perfectly level. The continual stops to discuss the merits of French wines, while eyeing up my wine rack, did not hold him back. Nor did the unbelievably long lunch breaks.

Plus, when it came to our first crisis he heroically stepped up to the mark or in this case nearly into the mark.

Basically, houses in remote French villages do not have mains sewage. They once relied on a cesspit, this was just a storage tank that held the waste products. This could be from your sink or loo-flush but did not treat the waste thus often needing emptying. Or for more recently built houses, a 'Fosse Septique'.

(A large tank that biologically breaks down waste solids and allows the remaining water to soak into the prepared ground.)

The cesspits could be outside in the garden but were often found somewhere inside the older houses. This could prove a bit of a challenge due to the interesting aromas!

Sometimes you could even come across folk, like another local guy called Maurice, who had no idea what sewage arrangement they were using. He only lived for two things, playing pétanque and hunting. His external sewage arrangements were somewhat of a puzzle to him and never even considered.

"Have you got a cesspit or a Fosse Septique?" I once asked him.

"Neither," he nonchalantly replied.

"You must have," I explained, "you must have something to get rid of the waste."

"No," he continued, "the pipes just go into the ground and disappear."

"But where do they go to?" came my rather puzzled reply.

He answered with the long established and often seen 'Gallic shrug'. You will continually see this in France. Basically, it goes like this:

1/ Arms close to the body and bent at the elbows at about 90 degrees.

2/ Both palms facing nicely upwards.

3/ Raise the shoulders as high as you can while tilting your head to the left.

4/ Pull a very unhappy face.

It is the classic French answer to a question that they do not know the answer to, do not care what the answer is, and probably had never even considered it worthy of thought.

Try it next time you get stopped for speeding and are asked by the police why you were going too fast........maybe not!

Back to the crisis at the farmhouse. We had a 'Fosse Septique' which if you remember was basically a very large tank sunk into the ground. I am reliably informed that the remaining soak-away water, after this natural biological treatment process, is almost drinkable......I suggest you take that on advice but never try it.

Quite quickly on our arrival this tank, that we had been informed by the owner never needs emptying, needed emptying. It kindly demonstrated this fact by overflowing into the shower tray in the ground floor shower room.

Now picture the scene, there we were 'Fosse Septique' virgins stood watching a large amount of brown sludge oozing up through the shower plug hole! To my wife's request as to what the hell was happening, I initially thought of just giving a Gallic shrug. However, I decided that this was not quite the right time for it as I actually wanted to carry on living.

Luckily I had been given the telephone number of Bernard, the village 'do it all', by Henri; but....and this is a big BUT...it was lunchtime. And as you shall discover in the next chapter nothing happens at lunchtime.

Now perhaps it was my panicked voice or perhaps just the fact that Bernard could not understand a word that I said, but he arrived immediately and nodded sagely. He knew what was going on.

The next moment he could be seen at the rear of the farmhouse sat with his legs dangling into the large 'Fosse Septique' manhole stirring the contents with a big stick.

He seemed quite happy with this and calmly chuffed on his cigarette whilst looking wistfully at the contents. This had the magical effect of stopping the sludge intrusion into the house. And he completed his task by ringing for the 'Fosse Septique' emptying lorry to come and clean out the tank.

I thanked him profusely but did wait until he had washed his hands before shaking them! I offered him a drink, thinking coffee, to which he replied that a large Scotch would be nice.

Several Scotches later he could be seen driving his van erratically back to base with a large, uncleaned stick protruding from the rear window. Strangely it was the clean end of the stick that was actually outside of his van!

Bringing all this back to the Mince Pie story; next to arrive was a large crowd who had obviously met up before arrival and descended on us 'en masse' as a safety in numbers strategy. Luckily one couple knew some words of English, that helped with the disjointed conversations.

Then suddenly in the garden a head appeared from the side of a tree, then it disappeared again. Then a different head appeared from the other side of the same tree then disappeared again. Finally, a head appeared from both sides of the tree and remained transfixed on the farmhouse.

It was, of course, Jean-Pierre and is wife Madeline. They were taking no chances and were making sure that a large number of French people had arrived before they would take a step inside.

Now I mentioned earlier that our guests were rather flustered as they had never been invited into a British house before. Well, think of poor Jean-Pierre and Madeline; they had never been invited into anyone's house before. And I have to say, I was a little bit concerned as I still had not worked out if the smell that radiated from his daily promenades came from the sheep or himself.

I am pleased to report that both he and Madeline smelled nicely of carbolic soap. *(A distinctive and never to be forgotten smell that I had not encountered for decades. Basically, the soap contained Phenol, a carbolic acid and I thought the stuff had been banned!)* Also, by the pinkness of their skin I would imagine that a scrubbing brush had been used somewhere in the process.

The first thing that fascinated them all was the evidence of two dog beds on the floor of the front room.

"Do your dogs actually sleep in the house?" came the combined, somewhat aghast request.

"Er! Yes of course," we replied.

"What, even at night?" they continued.

"Er! Yes of course," we responded.

"But how do you stop them jumping on the furniture?" they asked in complete unison.

"We don't," came our rather understated reply.

At this stage I don't think that we could have explained the truth regarding the fact that it was us that actually struggled to find space on the furniture. And at night they were not on the furniture...they slept on our bed. Our French neighbours clearly were not ready for such a revelation.

The French are really not like the British when it comes to dogs. Their dogs are either dyed pink and dressed in a tutu or chained to a post snarling at anything that passes. Another type of dog which we Brits struggle to understand are the hunt dogs.

These poor souls are left locked in small kennels for 6 months of the year with, for the most part, little exercise. Then in September when the 'La Chasse' *(the French hunt)* begins are expected to run for long periods. This normally without much rest as the hunt chases various wildlife around the countryside.

I questioned this many times and was always met with the same response. They are not pets; they are working animals!

What is even stranger is the fact that some of these hunters had pet dogs in the house with hunting dogs shut up outside! More of all this in a later chapter.

They then noticed the Christmas crackers which we had laid out with the nibbles, snacks, mince pies etc. Now you have to remember these were mostly simple French country folk and pretty much none had seen a Christmas cracker before. So, we had to demonstrate in great detail,...twice, how you operated the thing.

They attacked them with gusto which produced hats, gifts and jokes being spread haphazard around the room.

At this stage it became very clear to me that trying to translate unfunny very British 'jokes' into French would, not only be a bridge too far for me, but would have been a stretch for Mr Jackson!

After all, let's be honest, we generally have to explain Christmas cracker jokes to ourselves every year. So, I decided to ignore them.

(Thank God there was not a curly 'fortune teller' fish amongst the cracker gifts; there is no way I could have explained that one.)

It also became clear to me that Madeline, Jean-Pierre's glamourous wife *(same outfit as when we first met by the way)* had never seen nail clippers before. And by sheer chance the first cracker gift thrown her way was a pair of nail clippers.

Hard to believe I know but she had no idea what they were, or how you could use them. Luckily one of the other guests showed her what they were used for and her face lit up.

I have never seen anyone so pleased with a Christmas cracker gift in all my life, in fact I began to believe it may have been the first 'gift' of any sort that she had ever received. However, she then proceeded to clip her nails...all over our floor.

She then continued by trying to clip her hair with them and finally began to reach down to her feet! At this stage our horrified look had registered on the Mayor's wife and she stepped in to side-track Madeline on to the mince pies and other snacks. On asking me what the pâté was made from, I innocently said 'maquereau' (mackerel) as I had prepared this word earlier. This just brought on a large amount of laughter as this word has a double meaning in France. I had basically just told them that the pâté was minced pimp!

Conversations about Christmas day with the locals highlighted some interesting differences. It is clearly not as important in France as in the UK. The big Christmas family meal in France being 'Le Réveillon de Noël' *(Christmas eve)*.

This family occasion is a sacred tradition to the French and can last up to 6 hours. The perfect occasion to blow the food budget and to buy in a large range of expensive foods not normally eaten.

In fact, the word 'Réveillon' comes from the French word 'réveil' meaning waking up. The implication here being that you are going to be up for hours. Just to be sure that you have lost plenty of sleep, the French do this all again for the New Year's Eve 'Réveillon'. Or as it is often called in France 'La Saint-Sylvestre'.

Another noticeable difference, they are not so keen on Christmas cards. They tend to just send a very small number to far off folk who they have not seen for some time. Thus, our approach of sending a card to all the neighbours was greeted by bewilderment. Why didn't we just wish them 'Joyeux Noel' in person?...they have a point or are they just tight? Of course, being tight myself I happily used this as a good excuse to stop sending cards in the future.

What we actually eat during this festive season is also very different. We go for a massive turkey, they go for seafood platters and huge slabs of Foie Gras *(the fattened liver of a goose)*. By seafood platter I mean a large plate with mostly unrecognisable ... stuff! I am sure those 'Bulots' *(sea snails)* were still moving!

I personally prefer not to have to wrestle with my food to get it off the plate; but they seem to relish the challenge of chasing wriggling crustaceans around the table while chewing endlessly on tough bulots.

Also, Foie Gras is equally questionable, not for the taste as it is just a really rich pâté; but for the method used to produce this product. Without getting too graphic, the goose's liver is 'fattened' by force feeding corn through a feeding funnel three times a day until the liver is up to ten times the normal volume!

This charming process is called 'Gavage' and dates back thousands of years. Many countries have banned the production and sale of Foie Gras due to the intense controversy over the production method. However, in French law it belongs to the 'protected cultural and gastronomical heritage of France'. As usual the jury is out as to who is right or wrong.

They, of course, find our cuisine somewhat amusing. Take 'bubble & squeak' for example. Everyone loves a bit of bubble and squeak on Boxing Day, a great way of using up the endless supplies of the vegetables we all purchased before Christmas. And also a way to tackle the remnants of the overly huge turkey we all struggled to push into the oven on Christmas day.

Now think about how you could explain the concept of bubble and squeak with zero French language skills to a houseful of French guests. I think you get the picture.

After much waving of hands, gesticulations and pointing at vegetables we were faced by a sea of blank looks. They all think that Brits are mad anyway and this just confirmed it. The best way to test this yourselves is to initiate a game of charades with bubble and squeak being on the first card.

Coincidently, many years later when my French language skills were much more passable, I tried this bubble and squeak explanation again. It was met by the same response. How can a Nation that thinks it's fine to gnaw on a frog's leg not understand a simple fried veggie dish?

This first invasion of our house by the locals also produced the first slight embarrassment for me.

The dreaded kiss protocol 'La Bise'. The French really do love to kiss each other repeatedly when they meet up. But there are rules; the problem for Brits is that the rules are incomprehensible.

There can be two kisses, one on each cheek. Three kisses alternately on each cheek or even four kisses in similar fashion. But this range seems to change from region to region; family to family and even village to village.

Also, which side do you start with? This is also a variant on village, region etc. Plus, the biggest no-no of all, never just one kiss on the cheek, that is classified as rudeness of the highest order.

Now you might think that this would not present a problem; but picture the scene. You mistakenly think it's three, so you're going in for the third as your guest is turning away because it's two. Thus, you end up kissing someone's ear.

Or you think it's two, so you turn away only to have someone kiss the back of your neck because it was three. Worst of all you think it starts on the left, so in you go but it starts on the right, so you end up giving Madeline a big smacker on the lips!

Also, this is a very time-consuming process. Nobody arrives like in the UK with a wave of the hand and a jolly 'Hi everyone'. Oh no, here you work your way round the room saying 'bonjour or bonsoir' to each person in turn. This is completed while performing either 'La Bise' with ladies and children or a handshake between the guys.

In a room of 20 people this could take some time, and really does break up any conversation as every time someone new arrives this whole procedure kicks off again.

Then of course this laborious process starts all over again when everyone leaves. No wonder their traditional family meals last 6 hours, half of that is taken up with hellos and goodbyes.

In addition to this 'la bise' puzzle comes the 'Vous or Tu' complication. 'Vous', meaning 'you' of course in French, can be replaced by 'tu' between friends, family, children and bizarrely pets. However this is France, so it really is not that easy. Some interactions, where we would think that 'tu' would be used, use 'vous'.

This is normally due to some hierarchy issue. Also, when addressing a respected elderly person, the 'tu' often reverts to 'vous'. It's a minefield and even worse, when do you actually change from calling someone you know from 'vous' to 'tu'?

Luckily the French are adept at this 'tutoyer' *(address as tu)* game so you just leave it to them. The only thing you have to remember is that 'tu' is singular only, a group of friends are 'vous'.

Interestingly, you can use this 'vous/tu' scenario as an insult. Apparently calling someone you have never met before as 'tu' is seen as insulting and is often used by the French in cases like, for example, the dispute following a car knock incident.

Finally, the biggest insult of all. After falling out with a friend who you have referred to as 'tu' for ages, you revert back to 'vous'.

So, we survived our first French gathering but were soon to be confronted by the next confusion at this time of year in France. It came with the never-ending stream of people who knocked at the door with our calendar. How many calendars does one household need?

First it was 'Le Facteur' *(the postman)* and as the first of many I was totally unprepared. It went something like this.

"Do you want a calendar?" he politely enquired, while spreading out a large selection.

"Why yes, thanks, why not?" I innocently replied.

"Which one would you like?" he continued.

At this stage he offered across the gate a large stack of calendars with varying cover designs on offer.

"I'll take the one with the dogs thanks," I continued.

Handing over the aforementioned doggy calendar there now followed a silent pause as he waited for me to hand over some cash, and I waited for him to hand over my letters.

Breaking into some broken English *(he turned out to be married to a Brit)* he continued to explain that the sale of the Christmas time calendar was the traditional way for people to provide a Christmas tip to the bearer.

"How much are they?" I innocently enquired.

"Whatever you like," he countered.

This was a game of chess I was never going to win. Give too much and I would never know but give too little and my parcels and post would probably end up in a ditch somewhere. So, I plumped for 10 euros which seemed like a good deal to ensure the arrival of the post for a whole year. He seemed very pleased and wandered off.

There then follow a whole myriad of calendar bearers from the local football team to 'Les Pompiers' *(Local Firefighting Team)* and each seemed disappointed by my 5 euros offering; no doubt word had spread that Monsieur le Facteur had been given a tenner!

I later actually asked Brigette how much she thought was correct for the Christmas calendar sales pitch, she thought a few euros was fine. She nearly passed out when I told her that I had given ten euros to the postman. No wonder he had started calling me 'tu' after his tip!

Others that tried on this yearly sales pitch were wine sellers, fire extinguisher sellers and anyone else that could get in on the act. The wine salesman was easy to get rid of, I basically told him that I only drunk English wine. His look of utter horror was something to behold and he never came back!

We also had a new experience to tackle at the doorstep; the army. The village was next to an army training camp; and you would often see lost souls wandering about with maps that had no markings other than roads, but no names. As to why, I have no idea, but the result was endless knocks on the door by bewildered soldiers asking where they were.

What made matters worse for them was their dress. In summer they would be wearing full kit with massive backpacks in 40 degrees of heat. In winter they would be on training runs wearing skimpy shorts and a vest in minus 5 degrees. This came to a head one wintery night; it was late, dark, raining, and cold. In fact, it was freezing and there was a knock at the door.

Guessing who it might be I answered and there stood a very wet, cold and shivering soldier dressed in a pair of shorts.

"Where is the camp please?" he enquired.

Recognising the obvious word 'camp' I pointed up the lane and said, "two kilometres."

"Thanks," he responded through chattering teeth and with that he started down the terrace stairs.

I called after him and pointing to my car made obvious driving motions with my hands, this being an invitation for a lift. He smiled, shook his head and ran on. I looked out at the freezing rain and worried that he would be dead before he reached the camp so rushed down to get in my car. He had only been gone 2 minutes, but I couldn't find him, I just hope he made it okay.

Just to show the seasonal difference, one very hot summers day an officer called out from our gate as I sat on the terrace. He was in full kit, was sweating profusely and in obvious need of a drink.

"Can I fill my water bottle please?" he asked, while making an easy translation for me by turning his empty water bottle upside down and shaking it.

"Yes of course," I responded, indicating the external water tap under the terrace.

"Thank you," he said, while turning around and shouting 'ALLEZ' *(come on)*

Suddenly we were surrounded by 30 or more equally suffering soldiers all holding empty water bottles. They politely queued, filled their bottles and were gone!

One thing at our new location that was recognisable from our past English village experience was the building of a 'Crèche de Noël' *(Nativity scene)*. Now this should be an example of all the village coming together at this time of 'good will to all men'. Not in Loser, it was war.

The problem was that this particular village had been at logger heads for years over problems with the 'Comité des Fêtes'

(Basically each village has a committee who organise all village wide activities including the big event each year, the village fete. This committee is voted in on regular occasions by the inhabitants of the village and is run as an association for financial purposes.)

The previous Comité des Fêtes had been accused of...well let's just say creative accounting. After years of running successful events, taking large amounts of money on beer tents, running Lotos and selling meal tickets etc. they had accumulated....nothing, zero, zilch!

This had produced much-heated debates at village meetings with accusations running wild as no financial reports were forthcoming.

This resulted in a mass resignation of the Comité leaving the village with nothing. And worse still, as there was no money in the kitty nobody was willing to take on the role of a new Comité member. Thus, the village for several years had nothing; no fete, no functions in fact no get togethers at all.

Now you might think that this must be an isolated occurrence but think again. The same had happened to the neighbouring village some 5 km away, and 5 km in the other direction it was looking like the same thing was underway for similar reasons.

There is something about the French mentality that leads inevitably to conflict whenever people get together to try and organise anything. We were very soon to discover the real reason for this; the French are incapable of organising anything!

Luckily a small group of individuals had decided that the village 'Crèche de Noël' was sacrosanct. Thus they had recovered the previous Comité's 'Crèche' accoutrements from storage and had started the construction of a Nativity scene.

These accoutrements included dummies, stuffed animals, clothing and a crib etc. In fact, most of everything you would recognise from the Nativity scene in the UK.

Now, Loser sat on top of a high hill, almost clifflike, pushed high over a valley by some volcanic activity millions of years ago.

(Bizarrely embedded into this high rock formation, hundreds of meters above sea level, were the fossilised remains of sea creatures.

When I mentioned this amazing fact to one of the aging locals he shrugged and told me that he had never noticed them!)

So, the obvious site chosen for the 'Crèche' was a small cave high up the hillside. This cave had to be passed by anyone arriving at the village via the winding small country lane that basically formed it's rear entrance. Power was supplied by running a long cable from the terrace of someone's holiday home.....without permission of course; and work began.

The first sign of trouble came when a member of the now defunct village Comité angrily arrived on the scene. He grabbed the donkey's head claiming that this item was his and he had not given permission for anyone to use it. He was last seen strutting down the road, talking to himself with a donkey's head stuck under his armpit.

There followed a stream of equally angry ex-Comité members who extracted various clothing, polystyrene heads, a papier-maché sheep and an ancient pair of 'sabots'.

(clogs – it's where the word sabotage or saboteur comes from. One theory for this relates to the invention of the 'Jacquard Loom' which used punch cards to automate the textile manufacturing process.

This invention of course put textile workers out of a job. Thus, the rather miffed workers threw their wooden sabots into the delicate Jacquard machinery wreaking ...well...sabotage!)

As you can imagine this depletion of the basic requirements of a Nativity scene was causing a problem, but in usual stubborn French modus operandi they just cracked on as if nothing had happened. The completed 'Crèche' was something to behold.

Joseph now had a tailor's black dummy head; possibly historically correct, who knows? And was dressed in what looked like a curtain. Mary had an overlarge blonde wig and the baby Jesus was just a bundle of sheets as the actual baby seemed to have disappeared.

One of the wise men now had the polystyrene head of Michael Jackson and was holding up his gift of what looked like a long piece of string decorated with CDs.

All this was surrounded by the last remaining papier-maché sheep, who looked as though he had been somewhat wrestled with, and a model of a dog. He sat looked rather bemused covered in wool pretending to be a sheep and finally a donkey with no head!

Lit up at night, from a distance, it looked rather imposing and was visited by many folks from surrounding villages who stood open mouthed at the spectacle. The real reason for the large number of visitors was lost on the folks in Loser who merely put up an arrowed sign pointing proudly to the 'CRÈCHE'.

CHAPTER THREE

Shopping & Say It With Flowers

Sat equally minding its own business a short drive away from Loser was the small town of Caylus *(named after the famous board game)*.

Whilst our village had nothing left in terms of shops, this small place had just about everything. A bank, a small supermarket, some bars, a couple of restaurants and a 'tabac'.

(The small shop where you buy tobacco products, newspapers, magazines, stamps and most importantly Lottery tickets!)

Next came several 'coiffeurs', *(hair dressers; always loads wherever you go),* a 'quincaillerie' *(a hardware shop), a pharmacie (what we know as a chemist or pharmacy)* and of course the ubiquitous 'Marché' *(weekly market)*.

Now if you cast your mind back to the start of the book you will remember that we were sat on arrival with no diesel for the car. This was because no garage was open to purchase this rather essential commodity. We were very soon to discover that actually purchasing essential items, or any items for that matter, is not always easy in France.

The French are to commerce what Attila the Hun was public relations...not a lot. When General Charles de Gaulle was quoted as saying 'How can you govern a country that has 246 different varieties of cheese?' He clearly left out the bit that said, 'and how can you actually buy any of them?'

(By the way, did you know that he had at least 30 serious assassination attempts against him! Some people live a charmed life. Listen to this.

Nicknamed 'the great asparagus' at the military academy, probably due to his height. He became a platoon commander at the beginning of World War One and was involved in fierce fighting at the battle of Dinant.

Here he received his first wound, as he was hit by a bullet in the knee. In 1915 he received the 'Croix de Guerre' award but was wounded again, and in 1916 while leading a charge he received a bayonet wound to the thigh. This after being stunned by an exploding shell following which he was captured after passing out from the effects of mustard gas; phew!

He was imprisoned for 32 months until the end of the war, but during this time he had made numerous escape attempts leading to being moved to a high security prison.

The start of World War Two saw him in charge of a tank battalion, and after some successful attacks against the Germans he rose through the ranks ending with a Government appointment. However, he was forced to escape to Britain after the Pétain Vichy government sought an armistice with Nazi Germany. Thus putting him in danger of immediate arrest.

Whilst in Britain he continued the French cause via stirring radio broadcasts that led to the Pétain Vichy government declaring a death sentence on him. I do not know for sure, but I would guess that he just gave a Gallic shrug at that!

His future life in politics was always controversial with the 30 plus assassination attempts including a Napalm bombing, machine gun attacks and even an alleged poisoning attempt by the CIA.

After all this Charles de Gaulle died of a heart attack at home watching television! I wonder what he was watching?)

So, back to French shops, basically they are always shut. Three hours for lunch, all day on Sundays, on Mondays because they are open on Saturday, Wednesday afternoon because the schools are shut or for a myriad of other strange reasons that always catch you out when you are in the greatest need of something.

To be fair they always put up a sign explaining a reason for this lack of commercial activity, but this does not help someone who has driven miles to find the place.....well....shut.

I will highlight here some of the more usual reasons for non-activity. The next time you are on holiday in France you can cross them off your list and see who is first to get a full house. Don't shout 'Bingo' though, you are in France, so just shout 'Quine!'

Number one:

Congé Annuel – meaning I'm off on a holiday and can't be bothered to keep the shop open. In fact, everyone who works here is going off on holiday, so you're screwed.

Number two:

Fermé pour l'inventair – Meaning - I am shutting the shop because I want to count up all the aging items that have been on the shelves for decades. Or more likely, I'm out the back having a fag!

Number three:

Congé de Maladie – Meaning - I am not feeling so great this morning so I came to work today anyway, just to put up this sign to say that I am not coming into work today.

Number four:

Jour de Congé – Meaning - I have taken the day off and couldn't think of a good reason. Come back tomorrow.

Number five:

Fermeture Exceptionnelle – I hate this one as it catches me out every time. Basically meaning - there are exceptional reasons as to why the shop is shut but I can't think of one at the moment, so I put this sign up.

And finally, the classic for all really lazy French shop keepers.

Number six:

Fermée – Meaning - as you can see, we are shut, and I am not going to tell you why!

Just to add to these particular unplanned woes there are a whole variety of other events that keep the shops firmly closed. 'Jours Fériés' is one that always catches you out. These days are, what we would call in the UK, Bank Holidays. You know the day in the UK when we all go shopping. In France everything shuts.

To make matters worse you get caught out as these days can be any day of the week. No Bank Holiday Monday or Friday here. When the actual date arrives, that's the day off and there are about 11 of them!

So, if you haven't studied your postman's calendar carefully *(I knew it was worth a tenner)* off you go for a nice trip somewhere on a Wednesday only to find the place deserted and everything, and I mean everything shut.

The other challenge is avoiding the continual 'grèves' *(Strikes)* The French have the amazing ability to continually find something to go on strike about. And due to the strength of the unions these strikes are very well supported.

Plus they normally increase in size as the 'appeler à une grève' *(call to the strike)* spreads.

(I will always maintain that the French really could not organise anything, however, if there is one flaw to this argument it is the organisation of strikes. They are very good at it!

As I sit writing this chapter, they are on strike again. This time against the rapid rise in fuel prices since the start of President Macron's tenure. They are out in force stopping traffic at roundabouts countrywide, and in particular causing chaos in Paris while burning tyres and wood in the streets.

These items are set alight with petrol thus ironically exacerbating the very fossil fuel conundrum that they are all striking about! The irony, of course, is completely lost on the French.

As to President Macron, well he came in as the French 'pin up' boy who had the answer for everything but very quickly demonstrated that he had the answer for nothing. At the roundabouts signs are up declaring 'Hang Macron', 'fight the government gangsters' plus a very worrying 'Aux Armes Citoyens,' meaning, to arms citizens.

This being a line from the strangely worded French National Anthem that we shall cover in detail later on. All the time this unrest is going on, the French Gendarmes are sat beneath the 'Aux Armes Citoyens' sign sharing a bar-b-que with the strikers!)

I guess the best way to summarise the difference, between the British attitude versus the French, is the recent rise in the retirement age. In the UK a rise from 65 to 66 had everyone moaning. In France a rise from 60 to 62 saw them all out on the streets burning cars!

Again, for us Brits who perhaps do not watch much French television or find reading the French newspapers a challenge, these strikes can cause unannounced havoc. You suddenly find yourself with no petrol, roundabouts blocked, various public transports closed and the most annoying of all, air traffic control shut. Thus, stopping all flights over France.

So, if you have booked a holiday involving a flight you spend months sweating, hoping that flights will actually be available on that date.

Well, why not just keep watching French television? you may ask. Surely the news will highlight what is going on. Unfortunately not. Firstly, French television is dire, and I mean really dire. Repeats of Dallas, dubbed in French from the seventies, along with an endless stream of very dated dubbed stuff mostly from America. Endless gameshows that mirror exactly the gameshows seen in the UK and old films that are mostly dubbed in French.

The news reports seem to gloss over anything of interest and mainly focus on the private lives of French politicians. That is if you can understand the rapid-fire French that hits you as you try and concentrate.

So, the first thing most ex-pats do is get that satellite dish installed so that UK TV can be watched. The problem here of course is that once you fall into that scenario you never bother going back to French TV; even though it would in fact greatly help with your language skills.

Various French governments have tried valiantly to get around this 'not open for business' attitude but were always scuppered by the strength of the French unions. They are determined to keep actual working hours to a minimum and maintain the tradition of lunchtime being family time, thus long lunch breaks.

The fact that in most families both parents worked, usually miles apart, and the kids stayed at school for their midday meal was lost on them. The end result, at lunchtime most towns looked and still look like the Mary Celeste.

So, you have to plan your shopping carefully. No point going out in the morning as by the time you get there, park up and walk to the shops they will be closing for a three-hour lunch break.

Thus, you leave in the afternoon having carefully prepared your list of places that are shut anyway on a Monday or Wednesday or maybe Thursday. Then you finally get to your shopping destination only to find 'fermeture exceptionnelle' stuck up in the window.

The French themselves do not seem to be bothered at all by this shopping challenge. They pop out anyway in the morning, find a suitable restaurant and spend three hours having lunch before their actual shopping experience. Two hours of this lunch being taken up with 'La Bise' saying hello or goodbye to everyone who enters the place.

Once actually inside a shop the next challenge is getting out again. There are many obstacles to overcome when trying to part with your money in any French shop. The first hurdle will be nobody at 'La Caisse' *(the checkout)*. This is because the shop can only afford one person to run the whole place due to employer social charges.

These can run to about 50% of the employee's salary, *(the list is endless including family benefits, sickness, health, accidents, unemployment benefit, main pension and a complementary pension)* thus you will not find an abundance of employees anywhere.

It is also nearly impossible for a French employer to remove an employee; yet another reason to be very wary as to how many folks you employ.

So, there you stand with your purchase while the checkout person is somewhere else; or is talking to a friend, or is admiring the stack of tins that they have just piled up in everyone's way in the aisle! And when they do finally saunter over to complete your purchase do not expect a 'sorry to keep you', this is business as usual.

The next hurdle is the classic 'not enough people at the checkout'. Now I know you can get this anywhere, but in France it's an artform. This scenario is most evident in the supermarkets where you walk with your trolley towards the exit and find a choice of about 10-12 checkouts. Unfortunately, only two of them have anyone at the till, thus a large queue has formed at both.

Then all the customers proceed to pay with a chequebook, *(yes, that's right; while the rest of the world is into contactless payments with cards, the French are still into writing out cheques!)* with much fiddling, looking for a pen, signing and various questions to the checkout person.

Meanwhile that block of ice cream you picked up is now liquid and the fish is beginning to smell a bit.

Finally, there is only one person in front of you, but they turn out to be a friend of the checkout person and there follows a long chat about...well anything really. By the time you get out of the shop that nice bottle of Chateauneuf de Pape you bought to lay down for a special occasion is now past its 'drink now' date.

(Okay, hands up, one of the most satisfying things about living in France is the price of wine. It is cheap, very cheap.

You can buy a decent bottle of Bordeaux for about 3.50 euros, the equivalent in the UK costing you about a tenner.

However, if you are into new world wines forget it. You will simply not find them on the normal supermarket shelves; it's as if they do not even exist. The best you can hope for is a drop of Spanish Rioja, all else will be French.)

The final shopping hurdle is if you dare to enter any shop as their long lunch break approaches. We had the classic example of this in a large furniture shop where we had found the perfect chest of drawers for the main bedroom. The shop sold high quality furniture, but this was unfortunately reflected in the prices, this piece of kit was going to cost about 800 euros!

However, we decided to splash out and sought out the vendor. It took a while, but we finally found him reading a magazine on one of the display armchairs. The conversation went something like this.

"Bonjour, we would like to purchase the chest of drawers over there," I said.

"Bonjour Monsieur-Dame, not possible...sorry," he politely responded.

"Oh, why not?" I enquired.

"Because it's nearly 12.00," he stated, as if this statement was perfectly logical.

"But it's not 12.00 yet is it?" I hopefully countered.

"True, but it will be by the time I get the paperwork done," he responded.

"And that's a problem because?" I calmly continued.

"Because I go to lunch at 12.00; you will have to come back at 15.00," he casually replied. He had obviously had this conversation many times before.

"So, to summarise I want to give you 800 euros, but you will not take it because you want to pop out for a sandwich?" I replied, trying hard to keep cool.

"Yes, you will need to come back at 15.00," he repeated.

We left the shop stunned that a large purchase was just waved away because a sandwich was looming. He did however give us a jolly 'Bon après-midi' *(good afternoon)* as he ushered us out of the door. As he shut the door behind us the town church bells struck 12.00, just to rub it in.

The next day I had formulated a plan for all the DIY jobs needed at the farmhouse, so I set out for Caylus to check out the hardware shop. On arrival I was greeted by a handwritten sign on the door stating that it was 'Congé Annuel'. This time proudly declaring that this unannounced time off was going to last from today for three weeks; splendid.

Now it was 11.30 and by the time I had driven to one of the big DIY stores it would be 12.00, I think you get the picture; so, I decided to grab something to eat and a coffee.

Now one of the great things about France is that you can go into a café, just order a coffee and get out your own food to eat it. Nobody cares; unlike the UK where it would definitely be frowned upon. So first I went into the 'Boulangerie' *(bakers)* for a croissant to go with the coffee and a baguette for later.

After the requisite 'Bonjours' to everyone in the boulangerie and the normal wait while someone in front of me runs through the story of their life, I got to the till.

"A baguette and a croissant please," I requested in my best, well-practised French.

"No problem," she said, putting a croissant in a bag and handing over a baguette that must have been three feet long.

"Er! have you got a baguette that is a bit smaller?" I responded, in a series of strange hand signals and miming.

"No problem," she repeated, and simply broke the baguette in half, handed me one half and threw the other back in the rack.

It would appear that a request for half of something is quite common and that other half would have been quickly snapped up by a following customer. You will often see this in markets as cabbages, cucumbers or perhaps a melon will be chopped in half at the request of the purchaser.

These baguettes are quite interesting and if you have ever wondered why everywhere you go in France you see someone with a baguette under their arm; read on.

Baguettes do not last more than a few hours. If you buy one at 8.00 in the morning by lunch time it will be as hard as rock and totally inedible. So French folk are forever having to nip out to replenish their stock of bread. Now, if this hardening of their bread is a natural process, one has to wonder what they put in bread in the UK for it to last for days!

The other thing you will notice about baguettes is the number that appear to have no ends. It is almost compulsory to nibble the ends off these loaves on your way home. Called 'le quignon' *(end of loaf)* it was often broken off while still hot from the boulangerie. Our dog Fritz often helped in this process while checking out people's shopping baskets in the crowded markets!

On arrival back at the café I ordered a coffee. Now be warned, if you just order a coffee, what you get is a cup the size of an eye bath with some dark brown sludge at the bottom.

If you order a 'café au lait' or a 'grand crème' *(both meaning a coffee with milk. Just a tip, only tourists ask for a café au lait)* you get the same amount of coffee sludge in a cup the size of a bucket with lots of hot water and milk.

Therefore before ordering I explained my predicament to Lucille, the café owner, who by good chance spoke rather good English.

"What you need is a 'noisette'," she explained.

"What on earth is a noisette?" I enquired.

"Well, a noisette is what you would call a hazelnut," she explained, "smallish in size and a light brown colour."

So, I ordered my first 'noisette' and a few moments later out came basically what we in the UK would call 'a cup of coffee'; result. Put this to the test the next time you order coffee in France and for once you will not look like a tourist.

The next thing that I really like about cafés and restaurants in France is the ability to take in your dog. Nobody bats an eye at your pooch sitting under the table while you eat a meal. In fact, in some of the restaurants we have frequented, dogs have been sat on owner's laps taking the occasional morsel from the plate in front of them.

Now, this is not for everyone but if you are a dog owner the ability to sit anywhere for a coffee, without feeling like a pariah, is great. In fact, it is most usual for the waiter to bring your dog a bowl of water unrequested along with your purchases.

The worst thing about cafés and restaurants in France is the smoking. *(Now defunct and banned but when we arrived it was endemic.)* Lots of people in France smoke and they really do not care where they do it.

Picture yourself sat at a table inside a restaurant just about to start your meal. At the same time the people at the next table light up their cigarettes; and unfortunately these happen to be normally Gauloises.

(Actually meaning 'Gaul Women', a very French cigarette made of dark tobacco from Syria and Turkey. It produces a very strong and distinctive smell. Between the wars the smoking of Gauloises was considered patriotic and was linked to many famous names such as Pablo Picasso and Jean-Paul Sartre etc.

82

In fact, George Orwell tells how he 'squandered two francs fifty on a packet' in his book Down and Out in Paris and London.)

However, no point in moving tables as most of the other diners are doing the same.

As an ex-smoker I found this abhorrent. *(Nothing worse than an ex-smoker when it comes to smokers.)* The worst case being the eat-smoke-eat variety. They would light up a cigarette whilst actual eating their meal and between each mouthful take a long drag, exhaling the smoke while actually piling in the next forkful of food!

As laws changed and smoking became illegal inside cafés and restaurants, the smokers simply moved their activity to the outside. Nowadays, what was once a pleasure to sit outside a café with your drink in the sun, has become a game of dodge the smoker as you search for the table all on its own.

Having finished my 'noisette' and having paid my 'l'addition', *(The bill; instead of miming writing out some imagined thing when you want your bill in a café or restaurant, simply request 'l'addition s'il vous plaît'. It will set you apart from all the other visitors.)* I headed for the market. Unfortunately, on the way our dog

Fritz decided to do a dump on the pavement outside a restaurant

(I continually marvelled at his ability to dump either at an inappropriate time or very inappropriate place. His most famous attempt at causing offence was on the actual steps of Shakespeare's birthplace!

Fritz, by the way, was named due to him being a German schnauzer breed. This turned out to be a bit of a problem in campsites across France as there were always plenty of German campers. So, every time Fritz got loose, I had to walk up and down shouting FRITZ at the top of my voice. This nearly always started World War Three!)

I, of course, grabbed a doggy poo bag from my pocket and proceeded to scoop up the offending 'deposit'. The look of shear horror on the faces on some passers-by was matched by baffled look of disbelief on others.

Had that guy actually just picked up some dog crap? Another wake up call, dog owners in France are not very good at picking up their dog's mess. They prefer to just leave it on the pavement for others to 'discover'; or simply let their dogs roam about all alone to leave their calling cards wherever they wanted.

The concept of picking the stuff up for disposal in a more appropriate place didn't enter their heads. On one such occasion, while picking up Fritz's latest offering, a lady rushed out of a shop and I thought she was about to complain. But no, she thanked me profusely for bothering to clean up after my dog, an action she had never seen before.

To be fair, as time went on the French tried to turn this around by installing dog poo bag dispensers in most towns and villages. However, you still have to tip-toe along most pavements to avoid getting caught out.

The market in Caylus was small compared to most but was worth a browse. What is evident is the popularity of the French weekly 'marché' even though large supermarkets can be found everywhere.

They cleverly spread market days from village to village therefore ensuring that there is a local market to be found on just about any day somewhere.

However, what is also evident is the high price of everything. Local folks seem prepared to pay nearly twice the price of most fruit and vegetables in the market as compared to the supermarket prices. Mainly due, I would guess, to the freshness of the products. What is also baffling is the number of small local vendors who appear to have almost nothing to sell.

Perhaps sat against a wall with a few dozen eggs or a tray of potatoes. The clue here is that vendors like these pay nothing to sell their goods in a market. Thus, if you have had a glut of something from your own garden, just get down to the market and get selling. Bizarrely, I never saw Henri doing this.

The modus operandi for purchasing something off a stall was also interesting. Basically grab a plastic basket, roam up and down the stall throwing in various items then stand waiting your turn for the vendor to add it all up.

This of course requires the purchaser to press, squeeze, smell and generally size up each potato or carrot until the 'best in show' is found. I certainly would not have liked to follow Jean-Pierre at any of these stalls.

My reason for being here today though was not due to the urgent need for vegetables. In response to our 'drink and mince pie' evening, Henri and Brigette had invited us over for an 'apero'.

(Short for aperitif; in France this sort of invitation means a few drinks, a few nibbles, a lot of 'la bise' and bonsoirs. This will be

followed by talking about the villagers not present.)

We of course had done our research on what we should take. First mistake would be a bottle of wine. This is in fact a mild insult that suggests that the host serves up rubbish wine. So, we decided on flowers.

Now, this is also a minefield as some flowers in France like carnations are considered bad luck as a gift. Flowers such as roses are reserved for lovers only. Even numbered flowers can be bad luck and so on and so on.

However, at the beginning of November we had seen an incredible selection of potted chrysanthemums on sale and they were without doubt popular with the French; they were snapping them up. So, that was our choice.

Now we arrived late as per our internet guidance, went through the 'la bise' dance with the dozen or so guests already there and proudly handed over our chrysanthemum offering to Brigette. The room went quiet, very, very quiet. Jaws dropped, drinks on the verge of being swallowed froze in mid-air and all eyes turned to Brigette.

This seemed to last for hours as it slowly dawned on us that we had committed some sort of 'faux pas'; but of course, only a few seconds passed before the room burst into laughter.

The Catholic festival of 'Toussaint' *(all saints day)* is on November 1st. Traditionally in France this is the day when families all over the country take flowers to the graves of deceased relatives; and it is well respected. In fact, those folks who do not maintain these family graves can actually get into trouble.

Under French law graves must be visited and well maintained, if not notices can be placed on the grave itself, the town hall or cemetery entrance asking for an explanation. A zero response to these notices can result in repossession of the plot.

Concessions for grave plots in France can be purchased as a 'concession perpetuelle' *(In perpetuity)* or perhaps a 30-50-year duration. If these shorter durations are not renewed, the council can exhume the corpse and re-sell the plot. This is simply because of the fact that the number of these concessions are in very short supply.

A point well noted by the mayor of Cugnaux in 2017 who actually banned anyone from dying *(yes, you did just read that correctly)* in his commune unless they had a plot already reserved! This was done to highlight the lack of concessions available to his villagers. Just as a final point on French logic in this area. You are legally allowed to marry a dead person in France!

Thus, this flowering of graves on November 1st is a popular event. And it nearly always involves chrysanthemums. This started on the first armistice day in 1919 when the Prime Minister of France called for the French to lay flowers rather than the more popular candles on the graves of their fallen soldiers.

Chrysanthemums, being an autumn flowering plant, seemed the best choice and since then have been associated with death. Yes, you got it, we turned up at our first ever French invitation into someone home and presented them with a symbol of death.

An instant realisation that our gift was not in fact an insult, but a true error was met with much mirth. I guess we were not the first to make this mistake and will probably not be the last.

Another flower puzzle that hit us a few months later was the small potted plant that appeared on our terrace one morning. No note, no explanation just a small potted plant sat there all on its own. Rather puzzled by this we walked the dogs only to find our lonely plant had been joined by another. There were now two potted plants on the terrace.

Now what we had not realised was that this was 'Fête des Voisins' (neighbours' day). In 1997 Alanse Périfan had the misfortune to discover that an elderly neighbour had died in his apartment block without anyone realising this event for months.

He attempted to rectify this lack of neighbourly awareness by introducing a day each year when neighbours get together for a drink, snacks or simply give each other flowers. The following year this idea was taken nationwide and has since gone global.

Now this is where strange French logic kicks in. So, the idea is to give something to a neighbour each year to check he/she is still breathing. But our potted flowers had been left on the terrace without even a knock on the door. So, we could have been dead inside for months! Unlikely I know and a charming gesture but falling short on the original plan.

You will meet this odd French logic on many occasions in the book. In fact, after a few years of puzzled looks whenever our French friends did something very odd, we just gave a Gallic shrug and said, 'they're French'. That became the universal answer to everything.

CHAPTER FOUR

French Toys and an aging Lothario

Whilst sat on the terrace at the front of the farmhouse admiring the fantastic view across the neighbouring valley, I was somewhat struck by an incredible vintage car chugging up the road. It was a very old open-top Chenard Walcker that looked in incredible condition. I waved and mouthed 'bonjour' and the valiant driver pulled over for a chat.

"Just moved in?" he enquired, in perfect English.

"Why yes," I replied, "I must say, your English is very good," I continued.

"Always been a student of languages," he explained "German, Italian, English and of course French."

"Really nice car," I said, trying hard not to sound jealous.

"One of my best," he said, 'I collect them.'

I asked if he had many in the collection and he suggested that I pop round to take a look, as he lived just a few hundred meters down the road. His name was Ollie and unlike most of the locals here in Loser he seemed well educated and had obviously travelled extensively.

Aged about 68 he was always well dressed and looked incredibly fit for his age. He was small in stature, but this was made up for by his larger than life enthusiasm for everything. Be it cars, walking, talking and ...er!...women!

As we spoke another chap pulled up, wound down his car window and said in heavily accented English 'I am going to play tennis'. Both I and Ollie stood waiting for the rest of the statement but that was it. After a long silent, somewhat embarrassing pause he explained himself to Ollie.

Apparently at school he was made to say something in English at every English lesson. All he could remember was 'I am going to play tennis'. That was his full repertoire and he was not going to miss an opportunity to use this extensive knowledge. This of course brought back memories of my own language skills thus I completely empathized with his logic.

Unfortunately for years afterwards he would drive past our house, wind down his window and shout 'I am going to play tennis' at the top of his voice. In all the years I lived in the village I never had any other conversation with him.

This drive-by 'shouting' was also a trick of the village 'cantonnier', Marcel. *(Basically, the village handyman who mends roads and keeps the village tidy; a role paid for by the Mayor's office.)* He once asked me to teach him to swear in English. As to exactly why he wanted to do this I am not sure. I believe it was just to retaliate to the fist shaking tourists who he had nearly pushed off a lane by his usual driving style; down the middle of the road.

(You have to get used to the French approach to driving very quickly if you want to survive. Basically, they continually drive down small country lanes in the middle of the road playing 'chicken' with any oncoming traffic. You will need to budge over almost into the ditch; they will move over two centimetres and think they have done you a favour.

As I arrived in my right-hand-drive Land Rover actually judging the distance between my car and the oncoming offender was very difficult. The result of this was several broken left-hand-side wing mirrors. This was probably the main reason for changing to a French left-

93

hand-drive car as soon as possible, because Land Rover wing mirrors were not cheap!

Their other modus operandi is to move up behind you and drive very, very close until you give in, pull over and let them pass. Now, don't you worry that one of their indicator lights are not working as they never use them. Also get very used to the car horn; they use that all the time; for any reason.

For example, at the traffic lights you are sat there, and the lights change to 'GO'. By the time you have changed into first gear to pull away, the guy behind you is bleating his horn because you are 3 nanoseconds too late!

The other thing to be wary of is parking. Do not leave your car in a parking spot that has a space either in front or behind smaller than two car lengths. French drivers habitually see small parking spaces as a challenge, and remember they have no qualms about battering their own cars because...well....they are already battered.

I quote the classic example. We were sat in a nearby village café drinking a cup of coffee watching the world go by. In front of the café was a gap that I personally would have struggled to park a motorcycle in. An old white van pulled up past the gap, quickly reversed

94

into it hitting the car behind; thus pushing it a metre backwards.

He then moved forwards quickly hitting the car in front, pushing it about a metre forward. Happy with the 'now parked van' result he stepped out of his van and simply wandered off to do some shopping. Most of the folk in the café didn't even look up to investigate the noise. Those that did glance up simply carried on as if nothing had happened. This was normal!)

So back with Marcel the cantonnier, I naturally went for the good old Anglo-Saxon simple but effective "fuck off" which he annoyingly practiced continually. Everywhere he went he could be heard introducing it into conversation. No doubt many right-hand-drive British cars came under the bombardment of his newly found conversational piece.

All these chickens came home to roost once when my aging mother arrived to inspect our French purchase for the first time. As she got out of my car and looked up at the ancient pile that we called home, a very loud shotgun blast shook us all.

This was followed by an equally loud "Putain Merde Alors," followed by a shout of "FANNY" from Henri's garden. *(Don't panic, French swear words will be fully explained in a later chapter.)*

At the very same moment as my mother was nervously looking round to seek out the cause of the explosion, and the demand for Fanny; a car passed the house. From it came a shout of "I am going to play tennis!"

While she spun round to seek out the origin of this helpful sporting update; a French chap, who was busy clearing leaves from the road, waved and shouted, "Fuck Off'!" She turned to me ashen faced for an explanation, all I could think of was a classic Gallic shrug!

While I arranged to pop round to check out Ollie's car collection, a now recognisable aroma hit us. This was quickly followed by the sound of shuffling feet and Jean-Pierre appeared with his sheep. As usual most of the sheep were either limping or hopping, they didn't appear to have a good leg between them.

The sheepdog followed up the rear tightly connected to a long piece of rope. Now, unbelievably, Ollie was about the same age as Jean-Pierre and as a village local himself he had known him from childhood. He laughed when he explained to me that Jean-Pierre knew the names of all of Ollie's past girlfriends, a feat that Jean-Pierre proved by reciting them.

This was going on for some time and Ollie decided to stop him at about number 30!

(I actually think that Jean-Pierre was slowly approaching names that I might recognise, as I am sure a bead of perspiration had appeared on Ollie's forehead!)

"He knows everyone's car registration numbers as well," quickly interrupted Ollie.

"Okay" I challenged, "What's mine?"

Now I have to admit that I did not know what my registration numbers were, at this stage we still had one from the UK, one French and our UK caravan. He reeled them all off in seconds. I was a bit flabbergasted and even more so when he began to list off the registration numbers for all Ollie's vintage cars, most of which had not left his garage in years!

This guy might look like a tramp and apparently struggle to both read and write but his powers to memorise stuff was outstanding.

(I wish you were still around Sigmund Freud, what the hell is going on?)

As he wandered off muttering the car registration numbers for Henri, Brigette and the

Mayor; Ollie filled me in with some of his incredibly sad past history.

His father was a prisoner of war and returned home when it had finally ended a broken and emaciated man. Jean-Pierre was about 8 years old and still at school, a shy small lad with a stutter.

But with his father unable to recommence the farm work, Jean-Pierre was taken out of school and became the shepherd. His younger sister carried on at school and eventually became a school teacher herself.

So, the continual daily ritual of passing the farmhouse with the sheep had actually been going on for 60 years, even though Jean-Pierre himself only actually owned a portion of the estate.

(I will try and explain the complex issue of French inheritance laws a bit later.)

That afternoon I popped round to Ollie's house, well bungalow really, no, a very large garage with a bungalow attached. When he had retired from work, he had the place purposely built to house his car collection.

It's hard to describe really and only French logic would allow it to happen. Picture a nice bungalow surrounded by a picturesque garden and attached to the side of the bungalow a garage twice its size!

It had no windows so looked a bit like a squash court. However, its real purpose was clear as the large garage doors automatically opened. The first thing you saw was a huge hydraulic drive-on ramp that raises cars up so that work could be undertaken underneath.

Not one of your do-it-yourself types, this was a professional garage ramp. Next to that stood a huge professional oil extraction pump for changing engine oil. Surrounding these rather impressive bits of kit were a myriad of tools, cans and various bits of cars.

Then as the internal lights switch on you are greeted by a dozen or so very nice vintage cars. From the classic and much sought-after Citroen DS to the very expensive Jaguar XK 140. Sat in the corner was his Chenard Walcker next to an open top Panhard sports car. All of these cars looked in immaculate condition; well, all except one.

All on its own to one side sat a rather sad looking ancient black Peugeot. Covered in dust with one or two parts clearly being worked on, it had the strangest paint job I had ever seen. Basically, the whole car had at some stage been painted in black and white squares making it look like a chess board on wheels.

"Who on earth painted that?" I asked.

"I did," he proudly stated.

"Why would you paint an old car in cheque?" I enquired, it seemed almost sacrilege on an ancient car.

"It was my first car, I bought it second hand as a student and thought it would be fun to paint it like a chessboard," he explained. "Tell a lie; I paid my sister to do it, a few francs a square."

So here in his garage he still possessed the first car he had ever bought some 50 years ago. It was sat there waiting for a complete rebuild back to 'as new', a job he had been contemplating for decades.

(Just as an update, the last time I saw this car many years later it had been stripped to the last nut and bolt. It had then been sand blasted, repainted, rebuilt and looked as though it had just driven out of the factory.)

I asked him about the other cars, in particular the Jaguar which was stunning. He went on to explain that this one had been given to him by his father. Not inherited mind you, actually given as a gift. His father was still alive and had his own large collection of cars.

Basically, his father had told him for decades that he was too young to drive a car like that, thus he had to wait till his mid-sixties before he was old enough!

I was somewhat taken aback by the amount of money invested into this collection and wondered about his background. So, without being rude I simply asked him what he used to do for work. He explained that he was a travelling salesman, *(that explained a lot about the large number of girlfriends)* and he sold French cheeses across Europe.

Now as we know from Charles de Gaulle, France has about 246 different cheeses. So, I was interested out of this vast selection which one was his favourite. Without any hesitation he said 'Stilton', England's historic strong blue cheese.

I think my jaw dropped at this confession, but he continued with a quick request for me to bring some back from England the next time I went back to the UK. "You just cannot buy the stuff here," he confirmed!

(Now, whilst things have improved a small amount over the years, when we arrived finding anything that was not French in

supermarkets was quite a challenge. I have already mentioned the wine situation but the same went for cheese. You might find a couple of Italian cheeses amongst the vast hoard of French offerings. Or perhaps one, maybe two Dutch types, but British; No chance.

Now in truth since Charles de Gaulle's day it is claimed that the true number of different French cheeses reaches almost 1000. But, hang on, the British Cheese Board - I kid you not, they are actually called the Cheese Board. They either have a great sense of humour or are really dumb - state that there are 700 named cheeses in the UK.

So here we are, one Europe, a free trading entity and out of 700 UK cheeses French supermarkets stocked....none!)

The only obvious French car that seemed to be missing from his collection was the classic Citroen Traction Avant. *(Traction Avant, basically meaning front wheel drive.)* A car design far ahead of its time. It became well known in the UK by its appearance on the television detective series Maigret in the 60s. *(sorry youngsters, just google it)*

But its true fame came from its use by gangsters before the war as the perfect 'getaway' car. Most famously by the infamous Pierrot le Fou and his 'traction Gang'.

This was due to the new front wheel drive, innovative steering and the new low-slung suspension which enabled it to be thrown round corners at speed. The police quickly retaliated of course, with many being bought as police vehicles, thus negating the gangster's advantage.

During the Second World War this fact was not lost on the French resistance who chose this car as an obvious 'getaway fast' mode of transport. Leaving a white FFI marked across the bonnet. *(French Forces of the Interior)*

This only to find that the Gestapo quickly responded by using the car themselves. This time kindly adding a WH to the registration number to signify 'Wehrmacht Heer' *(Army Command)*. The Germans took these cars to many places during the war and many ended up in Libya and even some in Stalingrad.

Thus, there were many worried looks during the Second World War if a sleek black Citroen Traction Avant suddenly pulled up in front of your house. A scene I unfortunately managed to replicate later in this chapter.

(Just to prove how far advanced this car was; many of its innovations dated back to 1934 such

as front wheel drive, rack and pinion steering and independent suspension etc. They simply did not appear on another mass-produced car in Europe until the Mini appeared on the scene in 1959.

In fact, there are some who would argue that Sir Alec Issigonis, designer of the first Mini, 'borrowed' some of his ideas from the Citroen Traction.)

Now, I have always been a big fan of the Traction, in fact for many years when I worked in London there was a chap who imported them, and sold them in a square near to Liverpool Street Station. There were many lunch breaks when I would go and look them over and ponder that one day I might own one.

I told this story to Ollie who candidly told me that the car I was talking about was the Traction 'Legere' or light. What he was seeking was a good example of the big 6-cylinder version, with the then new hydraulic self-levelling suspension. However, he did mention that if he ever wanted a Traction Light version, he knew someone who had one for sale safely tucked away somewhere.

This piqued my interest, even more so when he confirmed that as far as he knew it was still in immaculate condition.

Now here's a thing, when you move to another country you do tend to throw yourselves into everything with abandon to become a 'local'. For me it started with the Traction, then came an old Renault tractor, then came an aging Mobylette moped, then a beret, then a striped tee shirt etc. etc. I think you get the picture. I did draw the line though at sporting a moustache like a dead rat that the aging French guys seem to love.

I always had an excuse for these purchases; the tractor was needed due to the large amount of grass in the adjoining field that needed cutting. Also, I needed to pull the trailer full of logs that every year I would be cropping. Of course, neither of these two events happened more than once!

The classic French moped would be needed to pop down to Caylus for our baguette, but again this had a drawback. The moped was the most unreliable mode of transport on the planet. It simply stopped working whenever it felt like it leaving me stranded. Now these things have pedals but trying to pedal a heavy moped, wearing a crash helmet, in 35 degrees soon put me off the thing. Like everything else it soon became scenery.

So back to the Traction, I was really interested and had the budget, so we arranged to go with Ollie to meet the folks who owned it. They were very elderly and obviously had not ventured out in it for some time. I could not believe my eyes when he pulled off the dust cover to reveal what could only be described as a showroom condition car.

Dated from 1953 it was produced near the end of the Citroen Traction lifespan. It was bought new by a young teacher in Caylus whose father actually owned the local garage. Shortly after she bought the car, she moved out to teach in Chad. *(Once part of French equatorial Africa, thus French being one of the spoken* languages.*)* Initially this was for a short period, but it ended up as years.

Thus, the Traction sat sadly gathering dust in the rear of her father's garage simply unused. This was clearly demonstrated with the provenance backed mileage. They had documents dating back 50 years that demonstrated every new part bought, every test, and just about anything that had ever happened to it. The test certificates included actual kilometres driven since new.

This car had only driven about 25,000 kilometres. That's just a few hundred for every year of its life. The inside was pristine, climbing underneath revealed bodywork that you could have eaten your dinner off of, and generally it just looked like a new car. So, we bought it.

Naturally you do have a bit of a learning curve when driving any old car. Even though this one was packed with innovation it did not have power assisted steering, thus large biceps were required. Plus, the gear change was not synchronised thus an element of timing and engine rev control was required. However, it was a fun drive.

Once seen driving it, very quickly requests came in from various folks who wanted it booked for their relation's marriage. I began to see pound *(or was it euro)* signs; I could actually earn money from this. But first I needed to get my 'Contrôle Technique' *(technical test of vehicle).*

Like the UK MOT test, French cars when reaching a few years old must undertake a test to ensure they are roadworthy. This must be done every couple of years and failure to do so brings on a whole host of penalties. In fact, a seller needs to provide a certificate no older than six months old to actually enable the sale of a vehicle to go through. So off we all went to the local garage to attempt a pass.

(Out of interest, recently the French government have decided that if you have a 'Véhicle de Collection' dated before 1960; you do not need the 'Contrôle technique'. This is as long as the car hasn't been messed with. So, in France you can drive an ancient car without

any 'unnecessary' tests such as brakes, lights, and exhaust etc.)

Now I must say I was a bit dubious here, this car was over 50 years old and had not been used much. Would it actually pass?

The mechanic was known to Ollie as a fellow vintage car enthusiast, but I also knew that these 'Contrôle Technique' tests were quite tough. He immediately had it up on the ramps and climbed underneath with a lamp. All I could hear was 'Putain!', 'Sacre Bleu!' and various other French mutterings. I turned to Ollie for a comforting nod, all I got was a Gallic shrug.

When he emerged, the mechanic beamed with delight and simply said 'magnifique', even I knew what that meant. All the rest of the tests went well, the car passed with flying colours and I was all set for my new marriage car business. Now you know why I bought a beret and a striped tee shirt!

I quickly learned that being the chauffeur for the bride at a French wedding was not all fun. Firstly, French weddings seemed to last for ever and ever and ever.

(A bit like their funerals really, they last so long that I eventually forgot whose funeral it was. Their dress code at funerals also came as a bit

of a shock, basically same as normal. For an
example when Jean-Pierre's mother passed
away. He turned up to the funeral wearing
pretty much the same as his daily routine.

I also could not get used to giving the corpse a
round of applause during the ceremony,
perhaps I just haven't had much experience of
all this!)

So, back to the wedding, having waited for what
seemed like 3 weeks for the bride and groom to
appear out of the church you need to lead the
'procession'. This basically means driving slowly
through various local villages bleating hard on
your car horn repeatedly. This is while a long
procession of other cars are following, all doing
the same.

So, if you have ever been puzzled why, on a
Saturday afternoon in France, you hear a
massive bleating of horns, now you know.

Finally, you have to argue your way out of
drinking large amounts of alcohol even though
they know you are driving home. This is while
watching as several people sprawl all over your
treasured vintage car as the wedding pictures
are taken.

It was while driving home from one of these
wedding events that I was hit by unexpected fog.

It was cold but I was wearing my thick black leather jacket so what could possibly go wrong?

Now, these ancient cars run on a 6-volt battery supply which equals a lighting system that is not too great. Also, the main headlight bulbs were yellow! Thus, I was travelling very slowly as I edged through the village fog to get home.

Unfortunately, at that same moment Madame Vay was also walking through the village on her way back from her allotment. Now, Madame Vay was 90 plus years old yet could still be seen each day walking to and from her allotment. This would be either with a wheelbarrow or a basket of vegetables.

On one occasion I even saw her push a motorised rotovator up and down her vegetable plot! A feat that I am not sure I could manage. She was always accompanied by her even older husband who did not actually know where he was. However, he faithfully sat on a wooden chair at the allotment watching her work.

Fate had decided that on this day we would meet head on. Me slowly emerging out of the mist in the black Citroen Traction Avant, dressed in a black leather jacket. Her slowly advancing in my direction peering ahead through the mist.

The moment she saw me her face changed to one of terror as she crossed herself and mouthed the words 'Mon Dieu! ... Gestapo'. Realising that she was having a bit of a 'throwback' here, I thought of winding down the window to reassure her that all was okay. But she had a spade over her shoulder and no doubt she would not hesitate to connect it with my head!

Therefore, I slowly moved on. As I passed her, she just glared into the car as I tried a valiant reassuring smile. She was still glaring as I drove further into the village and I breathed a sigh of relief as the mist finally swallowed her up. I am thankful that her ex-soldier husband was not with her that day because I may not have made it back!

All this 'marriage chauffeur' scenario soon became a bit of a chore. *(Just to be absolutely clear here, if you happen to be a French Tax Official. This was all done for free as a kind gesture to the 'Entente Cordiale'; honest!)* Therefore, I decided just to keep the car just for fun outings, always trying to avoid Madame Vay.

Just thinking back for a moment, she was walking back from her allotment through a deep fog with a spade over her shoulder. And, since that day I never saw her husband again. Just saying!

111

Another item from the list of classic French toys that quickly accumulated, was various farm 'stuff'. Well it was an old farmhouse, and when we arrived there were two huge rusting bits of kit in our adjacent field that I moved into the garden.

When I say I moved them into the garden, what I meant to say was our friend Ken moved them into the garden after being persuaded how easy it would be, and what great fun could be had. It wasn't of course, and it took him about a week to get over it.

They were originally horse drawn and after getting blank looks and Gallic shrugs from many of the folks from whom I requested information, I turned to Jean-Pierre. He knew of course, in fact he had probably used something similar himself. But with much waving of hands, pointing and repeating words much more loudly we were getting nowhere.

I eventually waited for Ollie to do a translation for me. One was a large rake the other for picking stuff out of the ground, that's all the information that I was ever going to get.

"What do you want them for?" Asked Ollie.

"Just as decoration for the garden," I explained.

"I know where there's some other stuff," he continued.

Now it was becoming very clear in France, whatever you are talking about, someone will know someone else who has one for sale. It doesn't matter what it is, it always happens.

"Okay," I said, "where is this other stuff'?"

"In my stepfather's garden," he responded. "he passed away years ago and it is now mine and my sisters."

This is another French lesson. No French villager has just one house; there will be family homes spread all over the place. They are mostly empty and unlived in for some time. The sad fact is that when someone dies things become very complex in France due to large families and disagreements as to what happens to inherited property.

Shortly after arriving we were presented with a typical example of this. Monsieur Bosse, a relative of the original owner of our farmhouse, popped in to say hello and insisted on showing us around the empty house opposite. It once was part of the farm and was lived in by his uncle and aunt.

Since his aunt had died it had remained empty for many years and only now was he considering selling it. He obviously thought that us rich English folks would want to buy it. He was wrong on both counts.

On entering the house, it was like walking into a 1940s time-warp. Cutlery was still laid out on the table covered in dust. Pots and pans were in a sink fed by a hand pump. A jacket hung on the back of the door and all the rooms had clothes and stuff in the drawers and cupboards. Very eerie and very typical.

(Now, I am going to gloss over this inheritance problem quickly as it is a very complex area, and a whole book would be needed to cover it completely. However, it is worth checking out as it is very French!

Any property governed by French inheritance law cannot be freely disposed of by a Will. That's correct, you cannot just go leaving your own hard-earned possessions to whoever you want. Even if you hate your kids and have not spoken to them for ages, you have no choice, they're going to get it!

There are basically two groups who are eligible called 'Héritiers réservataires'. First, your kids. Second, if there are no surviving descendants, the surviving spouse.

The size of the inheritance depends on the number of children, for example, three or more children get three quarters of the property. The rest, one quarter, being subject to any Will. If there is no Will, the kids get the lot but if there is a surviving spouse, they will get one quarter of the property and so on and so on. I think you can see that this is a complex nightmare.

Also picture the scenario where someone has been married three times and has children from each marriage. You really do need a Cray supercomputer to work it all out.

This is all the fault of Napoleon Bonaparte of course. The French revolution had brought in changes to make succession laws fairer and understandable for all. Napoleon built on this and introduced his famous 'Code Civil' which ensured that children inherit both the rights and liabilities of their parents on their death. And unbelievably France still operates this same law centuries later. No wonder it is illegal to name a pig Napoleon in France!

While we are at it, something else to blame on Napoleon. He once ordered the lining of French roads in Plane trees to provide his marching troops with ample shade. You see this literally everywhere you go in France. However, since the invention of the motor car there have been

many fatalities by people crashing into them,
your fault Napoleon!)

So, if you have ever wondered why there appears
to be so many empty old houses across France,
especially in rural areas, the answer is that
descendants could probably not agree on what
do with the family home.

Some wanting to sell it, some wishing it to
remain in the family others missing and
impossible to find. Thus, there they stand,
empty, unlived in and crumbling away.

Returning to Ollie's offer to extend my French
agricultural mechanism collection, we popped
round to take a look. There in his stepfather's
garden, overgrown by weeds lay two large metal
reversable 'Charrues' *(Metal ploughs).*

These would have been pulled by a horse, in fact
one of them still had some spare horse shoes
attached to the side. We shook hands on 50
euros *(bargain I thought)* and all I had to do
was think of some way to get them back to the
farmhouse.

Now this is where living in a small village in
France can be a bit puzzling at times. While I
was contemplating how to shift this very heavy
equipment. *(For a start I didn't have a horse.)* I
decided that Henri might be able to help as he

had a tractor with a huge movable lift on the back.

As I walked over to his house to ask for help, he drove out with his tractor and waved me over.

"Jump in," he said.

"Where are we going?" I asked.

"To get your charrues," he answered, as if this was completely obvious.

I hadn't told him, and Ollie swore blind that he didn't tell him either, but he knew. Everyone in Loser knows everything about everyone else all the time. It is impossible to keep a secret in this place.

The first proof of this came when the lady who delivered bread in her little van each day had an affair with the guy who made cheese. Everyone knew almost immediately. So, a marriage of bread and cheese; that had everyone laughing. Of course, this would not have worked in the UK, you would have needed a third person who made butter!

The absolute proof came when months later I took my 'chasse' examinations. I scored 100% and was well pleased and couldn't wait to get home to show off.

As I drove into the village Marcel, the cantonnier, called me over, shook my hand and wished me 'felicitations' *(congratulations)*. Rather puzzled I drove on towards the house only to be stopped again, this time by Maurice; "felicitations," he said!

This was about 30 minutes after I had been told the result myself in a town some 20 kilometres away, yet everyone in Loser seemed to know the result already. I began to believe that they had known the result before I did!

Like all the other 'boy's toys' I slowly added to the collection, but many years later I decided to sell them all. On finding out that I was selling the old farm equipment, Ollie popped round and put in a bid for some which I gladly accepted.

"What about those two charrues?" he enquired, "are they going as well?"

"Why yes," I responded, "everything is going."

"I'll give you 100 euros for them," he said.

At this stage it suddenly dawned on me that he had completely forgotten that many years before he had sold them to me. And here he was now offering twice the original price to buy them back.

But this is France, and nothing makes any sense, so I agreed the price and he was now the proud owner of two horse drawn ploughs that he had already owned once before!

Ollie was not the only local guy interested in farm machinery though. Most days a young chap drove past the farmhouse chugging along on an ancient tractor. Unbelievably it was a Porsche..! I had recently bought my old Renault tractor dating from 1963 but had never heard of a Porsche tractor; I thought they only made sports cars.

(In fact, Prof. Dr. F Porsche had started work on his 'Volk-Schlepper' (people's tractor) in the 1930s. About the same time as work had started on his 'people's car'. The early models had been petrol driven but by the early 1950s the Porsche Diesel Tractor was in production. Several models were manufactured in different sizes from Junior to Master and continued until the close of production in 1963.

So, the next time someone boasts to you of driving a Porsche, simply ask them which model of tractor they've got!)

Seeing me messing with the Renault one day the young chap pulled up and we had a chat. He was interested in all things regarding agricultural machinery and even had his own little museum based in an old barn on their farm.

His father and grandfather were farmers and they belonged to the rather reclusive Garren family. In fact, Ollie had told me that he had rarely spoken to any of them himself, even though he had grown up in the village.

This quick chat led to a visit to see the Garren collection. What I did not anticipate was the number of old tractors that they actually owned. On arriving, there were 4 excellent condition Porsche tractors all in a row and all in working condition. He explained that as each model came out in the early 50s his grandfather upgraded to the new model. They were a stunning sight.

"Wow!" I said, "which one was the first that he bought?"

"Oh! None of them," he replied, "the first one is in the other barn!" Priceless!

Another toy, that was at the farmhouse when we arrived, was the swimming pool. Now on moving to the south of France I had quite fancied having a pool and this was, for me, a big plus with the house purchase. Very soon though you begin to learn the truth about swimming pools.

They are hard work, expensive and become completely undesirable unless of course you are a guest. For all the folks that came to visit I am sure it was great fun. A nice big, warm and clean swimming pool to relax beside taking the occasional dip.

For me, my life had become 'The Pool Man'.

(I did successfully brainwash my friends into believing that cleaning the pool was good fun and needed a certain expertise. Thus, whenever they arrived, all I had to do was just let them get on with it!)

It was a constant struggle during the summer to keep it clean with continual leaves and debris to clear out. Every day meant checking and double checking the chemical content else it would turn green very quickly in the heat.

Legal requirements meant it had to be covered over when not in use for security. Plus, an insulated cover was also used at night to try and retain the heat that had built up during the day. An alarm had to be fitted and maintained to sound off if anything hit the water by mistake, and so on.

When first opening it up, after the winter lay off, several attempts at cleaning had to be made before you could even see the bottom. In the autumn it could fill with leaves in minutes. And some rain storms could leave a large sand deposit slowly sinking before your eyes.

To winterise it was also hard work, draining water off, adding special chemicals and fixing the heavy winter cover. All this for just a few months splashing about. I think by now you are getting the picture. It really was not worth it.

Even if you heated the pool *(At great cost I might add.)* you would probably only use it for four months of the year and for those who just relied on natural solar heating, maybe two months of the year. So, there is a clear warning here. If you are contemplating buying a property with a swimming pool, either don't or quickly turn it into a fish pond!

The swimming pool did however provide another insight into the French commercial psyche. We decided that we would like some stairs descending into the pool rather than the metal pool ladder that was already there.

Also, the pool liner *(basically a very thick rubber liner that was manufactured to the exact internal measurement of your pool)* had a few repairs. Therefore, a new liner was ordered. These were not cheap, about 5,000 euros, however they came with a long guarantee, so we ordered one from a professional pool installer in a neighbouring village.

He arrived on time and set about his work. The old liner was ripped out leaving me with some of the best 'bâche' *(tarpaulin)* that I have ever owned. He worked hard to construct a stairway in concrete leading down into the pool base. He then took ages levelling off the floor of the pool as he was not satisfied with the old finish. And finally took numerous measurements to ensure that the new liner was a good fit.

He set a date for the new installation which was kept to the actual agreed date and time. He arrived and worked hard to install the new liner, this time with a colleague. He even repaired a broken timer that I was going to replace. He told me that he would be in touch with the final bill and left....not to be seen again!

Now, he had outlaid for all the materials and had not asked for anything up front. I had left several messages for him to send his bill without any response. So, I waited and waited then forgot all about it.

Roughly 18 months after he had completed the work there was a knock on the door and there he was.

"I have your bill for the pool," he casually said.

"Certainly," I responded, "I was expecting this some time ago."

"Been busy," he explained

So, I paid by cheque, shook his hand and with some thanks and good afternoons he was off again. This was typical of the 'laissez-faire' attitude of some of the French artisans. He had outlaid a large amount of money to buy the materials, yet had left it 18 months before bothering to come and collect his money!

CHAPTER FIVE

Pétanque and Swearing in French

There are some things that French folks are very passionate about, in the south of France it was playing pétanque *(a boules/ball game)* and the chasse. *(the classic French hunt)*

When I say passionate, I mean really passionate, therefore the two activities are carefully organised so that as the season for pétanque ends, so the chasse season starts. And, of course, as the chasse season ends the pétanque season commences again.

As you will read in this book, I became involved with both, and in true French fashion was treated to much organisational mayhem the more involved I became. It is worth analysing the game of pétanque before describing my 'apprenticeship' to give a better flavour of what I was up against.

It is one of many boule sports along with raffa, bocce, boule lyonnaise, and of course better known in the UK, lawn bowls and crown green bowling. Historically these types of games date back to the Egyptians where stones were used as the throwing object.

However, when cannons became a popular defence tool, cannon balls could often be found stacked in large numbers. These were originally about the size of a cricket ball. Thus, naturally it didn't take long before bored soldiers started playing around with these handy objects, and many types of game evolved.

Actually this game playing was not exclusive to France and paintings exist that depict Sir Francis Drake, and his followers, lobbing what appears to be a cannon ball onto a gravel surface. A game he famously insisted on finishing before laying into the Spanish Armada.

In fact, there appears to be some evidence that Napoleon Bonaparte himself tried to ban his troops from playing boules with the cannon balls. This was because they were more intent on finishing games than doing much anything else.

The very simple objective, with the game of pétanque, is to score points from your opposing team *(one, two or three people)* by leaving your 'thrown boules' closer to a target. *(A much smaller boule called the 'cochonnet' or piglet.)*

This point scoring being after both team's boules have been thrown.

The desired result is achieved by throwing your boules close to the target either direct, off someone else's boule or even by knocking an opponent's boule out of the way.

All this must be achieved while both of the thrower's feet are on the ground inside a designated circle. As this game is normally played on dirt or gravel this circle is usually drawn into the ground with your finger.

The very fact that it is played on dirt or gravel explains why you will see this game being played everywhere you go in France. In fact, be careful where you park your car next time you pull into a small village car park. You may return to find a group of players lobbing heavy metal boules all around it. And they really do not care too much what is in the way!

So, there you have it; pétanque in a nutshell, simple game isn't it? Well no; this is France so everything becomes complex and subject to much argument. In fact, the rule book for this simple game runs to some 70 pages!

Pétanque itself started as a game about 1910 as an offshoot of the very popular game of boule lyonnaise. The idea being to reduce the size of the playing surface by ensuring that the ball thrower remained stationary. Therefore, it was originally called 'Pieds Tanqués' *(feet planted)* eventually shortened to pétanque. And after development of the standardised metal boule it rapidly spread throughout France, then Europe and eventually the world.

However, this is France so there has to be some oddities. The most bizarre being kissing the Fanny!

When a team wins a game without the opponents scoring any points *(13-0),* the losing team is said to have made a Fanny. This can be 'Être Fanny', 'Il a fait Fanny' etc. etc. The consequence of which means the losing team must kiss the bare bottom of a girl named Fanny. This normally being represented by a picture, wood carving or perhaps a pottery figure of a bare bottomed young lady.

One version of the history behind this legendary activity states that Fanny was a waitress at the Café de Grand-Lemps, just after the First World War. She was so kind hearted that she would allow losers of a pétanque match to give her a kiss on the cheek.

One day the Mayor, who she disliked, lost and walked up to claim his prize. Instead she turned, lifted up her skirt and offered her other cheeks instead. A challenge that legend tells us the Mayor took up without hesitation!

This 13-0 loss scenario also has the unwanted impact of the losing team buying a round of drinks. And you will often hear 'Fanny paie à boire' *(Fanny pays for the drinks)* being called out. The drink of choice is nearly always a Ricard and large amounts of this drink will be consumed during a match.

If you want to explore further information on this strange kissing the Fanny ritual, I suggest that you 'google' it. However, be very careful how you word the search!

(Ricard is one of the many pastis drinks that you will find in French supermarkets. Pastis is a strong French aniseed and liquorice flavoured liqueur, somewhat similar to Ouzo or Arak.

Ricard is the best-known brand and in fact owns the second-best known brand, Pernod. It has been for decades the most prominent supporter of pétanque tournaments and events. So much so that ordering a pastis in any bar in France pretty much necessitates ordering a Ricard, all else being frowned upon.

If you have never had one, you will get a smallish glass with about half an inch of Ricard at the bottom. You will also get a small carafe of water which you will pour into the glass of Ricard.

Normally the ratio is about five parts water to one of Ricard. The result is a magical transformation as the drink changes to a milky, yellow colour with a strong aniseed aroma.

Note, it is unheard of in France to mix this drink for someone else! I once made the classic mistake of mixing large quantities of water with Ricard and then swilling it down like lemonade. What I forgot was that each glass of my bogus lemonade, throughout that very hot day, also contained Pastis. I ended up very drunk.

An elderly French friend explained the error of my ways succinctly. Always mix your Ricard to a strength that cannot be gulped but must be sipped. Else you are screwed.

The drink has a dubious past being a derivative of the older drink, absinthe. This aniseed based, very highly alcoholic drink was very popular in the 19th century. Particularly amongst artists and writers; most famously so Vincent Van Gogh.

Portrayed as a very dangerously addictive menace it was banned in much of Europe,

including France, in 1914. Now at that time
Pernod was the most popular brand of
absinthe, and after its ban quickly moved on to
the still legal, less damaging pastis.

Thus, the aniseed drink continued as we know it
today. Absinthe, by the way, has of late made a
comeback in less lethal form, and you will find
it on the supermarket shelves once more!)

So, in my rush to join all things French it was
clear that I had to take on this game. And like all
small villages it was played continually, all over
the place. But there was always one old chap
who seemed to be involved and he was good,
very good.

But he did have the annoying habit of
continually explaining to everyone where they
were going wrong. His nickname was, for
obvious reasons, was 'Le Professeur'. *(The*
Professor; this just meaning the teacher in
France.) However, I quickly cottoned on to the
fact that this nickname had an ironic element as
most of his interruptions were very much
unwanted. A fact completely missed by the
Professor himself!

He was in his early 70s and was the spitting
image of Father Christmas. With white hair,
white beard, big belly and a rotund always
happy face. For a joke I once pointed to him,

when my grandkids were visiting, and told them that it was Santa on a day off. They actually believed me and stood in awe every time he passed by.

It was no surprise when he turned out to be the village choice for 'Père Noël' in charge of giving out gifts to all the kids at their Christmas party.

It appeared that he was the partner of the Mayor's mother thus making it easy for me to introduce myself. It also highlighted a clearly emerging trend in this small French village. Not only did everyone know everything about everyone else; they all were related in some way to one another. Everyone I met seemed to have some blood relationship with someone else in the village.

After a brief chat with the Professor it was clear that the first thing I needed to do was buy my boules. This must be an easy task surely? Well actually no, it was a complex nightmare like everything else in France.

On arriving at the sports shop and locating the large pétanque section, I was confronted by a huge selection of different boules. Different sizes, different weights, different colours, different markings and so on. Where do you start?

I stood staring at the selection for some time before wandering over to the 'caisse' for some advice. Luckily one of the young servers spoke some English which probably saved me from making a daft choice.

(It was becoming very embarrassing how, just about everywhere you went, you could find someone who spoke some English. Why is it that most Brits cannot put more than a few words together in French, yet large numbers of folk in France can tackle a few sentences in English? I personally blame Mr Jackson!)

The first puzzle was his request to know if I was a shooter or placer. My completely blank look confirmed his first impression that I was either very dumb or a complete novice. Knowing that I was English he went for really dumb.

So, my first lesson then, you do not just throw these boules about. They are either perfectly placed or shot at an opponent's boule to knock it out of the way. Therefore, your leaning in one direction or another dictates the type of throwing boule you need. Smooth for shooters, grooved for placers.

As a novice, and understanding that the shooter's role was somewhat specialised, I went for the placer variety. This cut the selection by fifty percent. Next came the selection of the size and weight. This time you are helped by a large selection of boules to pick up, practise the throwing process, and check their suitability to the size of your hand. There is even a hand gauge to help in this process.

Next comes the number of grooves etched onto the boule; really, am I really still in this shop? I only came in to buy a metal boule. It's beginning to seem like years, they will be shut in a minute for lunch and I will be thrown out!

The number of grooves have two uses. First, the more grooves you have, the easier it is to use a backspin to stop the boule on impact with the gravel. Secondly, when there are three in each team and they have all thrown their boules, actually finding yours can be a bit of a tricky task.

Picture the scene; all the boules have been thrown and six people are desperately sorting through a dozen boules trying to find their own. Picking one up at a time and closely inspecting it. Looking accusingly at the boules that have already been picked up by their opponents.

Holding one up to the light before casting it down again while reaching quickly to snatch another out of their opponent's hand for examination. It was always chaos. So, remembering how many grooves were etched on your set of boules helped considerably.

I quickly came up with an obvious solution to this 'hunt the ball' conundrum. I simply put a red cross on each of my pétanque boules with a permanent marker. This was greatly frowned upon by all the other players who noticed it. With much shaking of the head, tutting and a few Gallic shrugs.

After a while though they came to the conclusion that this was in fact a good idea, so they all copied my innovation. They all also put a red cross on their pétanque balls. Thus, we all ended up back to square one again!

Back at the shop, next came the selection of colour. Well this was easy, all the colours other than steel were incredibly expensive. Therefore, steel it was. By now I was knackered, but my helpful assistant was only just starting.

"You will need a boule case, some cochonnets, a counter, a magnetic lifter, a measurer and a duster," he calmly explained.

"A what?" I said, again looking blank and calmly fingering my pocket to check that my wallet was still there.

Well okay I understood the boule case and yes, I will need a cochonnet/piglet but the rest?

"More than anything else you will need the measurer," he said, "and the counter will stop arguments," he continued.

So out I walked from the sports shop in a bit of a daze. Keeping me balanced upright were two large carrier bags filled with the accoutrements required by a simple game of throwing a ball!

This is another lesson in France, wherever you go you come back with a large amount of carrier bags. The classic example of this is if you dare to go into the pharmacie to ask for something for a cold.

'Certainly', will come the immediate response. Following this, one product after another will be piled up on the counter. Not for you to choose from of course, you are going home with all of it. So, out you pop with your common cold and two carrier bags full of 'appropriate' anti-cold products.

This is always the case with the French pharmacie even if you go via your doctor. A quick visit to the doctors with a suspected case of flu again sees you struggling out of the pharmacie with several bulging carrier bags full of stuff. You end up with a medicine cabinet at home with more products than Boots.

I was soon to discover that nobody else had hardly any of this 'definitely required' pétanque equipment. And the things like the counter were passed from hand to hand for perusal like some strange alien-based invention.

It was just a simple pocket-sized plastic device that counted two teams up to 13. This to ensure that there could be no arguments as to the continued score. However, all it really did was to create arguments as to the validity of the score on the devise; once everyone had forgotten where they were.

As to the rest, well for a start nearly every French pétanque player turns up to the game carrying his boules in a sock. Not a nice Marks & Spencer type but usually an aging woollen style with a few fashionable holes. This also doubled as the duster to keep the boules clean.

The only players with a magnetic 'pick-up' string were guys aged 90+ who found bending down to pick up boules impossible. For a measurer they made do with pacing out distances with their feet or picking up a nearby stick to use as a distance checker. As for the 'cochonnets', or 'piglet', well there were always loads about anyway, so mine stayed pristine in the case.

This was in fact the classic case of 'All the gear; and no idea'. However, I guess that over the years I used all this stuff eventually and never had to buy anything again.

The Professor was quite impressed when he saw my haul and suggested that we start by practicing on the gravel drive in front of the farmhouse. It all started out okay with me throwing and the Professor tutting and shaking his head. But very soon we were not alone.

My apprenticeship had only lasted ten minutes before Henri came wandering over with a sad looking sock filled with boules dangling from his hand. A further ten minutes in and Maurice pulled up on his bicycle to hang over the garden wall pointing, shouting to the left or maybe right before finally joining us.

A spare set of boules were recovered from the Professor's car and suddenly there were two teams battling out in earnest. I learned several things from this first attempt at this simple game. Firstly, there is definitely no such thing as a friendly game of pétanque. Very quickly these long-standing friends were arguing about everything.

Secondly, knowing a full range of French swear words was an absolutely requirement of actually playing the game. Thirdly, you must never start one of these matches without having a large supply of Ricard in reserve.

The problem here was that the more the Ricard disappeared, the more the swearing and general disagreements increased. Plus, interruptions from the Professor became more and more annoying. Including making Henri stand properly in the circle every time he threw his boule.

At one stage Maurice was on his knees carefully measuring the distance between his boule and the piglet, a distance that Henri had just disputed and measured. Meanwhile Henri was disputing the actual accuracy of the tape measure and was using his feet to compare the distance.

At the same time the Professor was instructing me on the technical advantages of putting backspin on the throwing boule, while both Maurice and Henri multi-tasked by disagreeing with him.

My head was spinning from one 'connerie' *(foolishness)* to another and I was starting to regret the whole thing.

However, my knowledge of French swear words was increasing by the minute with several being repeated over and over. 'Putain!' was their favourite, followed closely by 'Merde!' and plenty of 'Zuts'.

It is worth breaking off at this stage from the impromptu chaotic pétanque match to analyse some of the more useful swearing terms. However, please note I am not holding back here and some of the French 'Gros Mots' may be very offensive to some.

So, if you feel you may be offended or have no need to swear like a French trooper then you may wish to pop along to page 145 where you can pick up on the pétanque story again.

What I will do here is pick up on some of the more popular expressions with their meanings; but please note, this list is by no means exclusive. That would take a very large book all on its own.

Most people would have heard of the word 'merde' meaning shit, and for some it is probably the most understood swear word in the French language. In fact, its fame dates back to Waterloo where one of Napoleon's generals was heard to scream 'MERDE!' when he realised he was outnumbered.

(I wonder if this was just before their expertly performed military retreat from the Prussians, Monsieur le Mayor?)

So simply saying 'merde' is an equivalent to saying 'shit' in the UK. To extend its strength just a little bit just add 'alors', making the very useful 'Merde Alors!'. To take this one stage further add 'putain' to make Henri's favourite expression when something goes horribly wrong 'Putain, Merde Alors!'.

But, as in most cases in French, 'merde' is not the only word for shit. 'Chier' being a good example, meaning 'to shit'. So, if you see someone in France experience something surprising don't be offended if 'Fait Chier!' is the exclamation used.

Perhaps the most popular and most flexible swear word used in France today is 'putain' literally meaning whore. But it is actually used as the equivalent of the good old English word 'fuck'. Thus, it can be used in a similar fashion either on its own, as an exclamation, or combined with other swear words to strengthen their impact.

Those who follow Gordon Ramsey on his various cooking programmes will often see him mouth 'putain!' every time something goes very wrong. *(He learned most of his craft in France)* If you haven't noticed it just watch him carefully on the next programme.

So, it can be just 'putain!' or maybe 'my putain car is broken down', or 'this putain game is rubbish' and so on. Then to strengthen another swear word just add accordingly. For example, 'Putain de Merde!' when you are angry or even 'Putain de Bordel de Merde!' when you are really angry.

'Bordel' simply means a brothel but it is used as a minor swear word to express something that is a complete cock up. Once, when I was calmly sitting in a doctor's waiting room to receive my prescription for two carrier bags of products from the pharmacie; an English chap decided to show off his command of the French language.

Now I have to admit that things were busy, each patient was taking ages *(yes folks, no time limits in France)* and nobody knew who was next in turn. The chap declared in a loud voice that this was a 'putain bordel', unfortunately just as the doctor emerged to grab the next patient. The doctor threw him out!

Some other minor less-offensive expressions can be the ever present 'Zut' meaning darn or damn. Or maybe the occasional 'Oh la vache' meaning holy cow.

We move now to some of the stronger expressions so brace yourself. If you remember, Marcel the cantonnier had asked me for an

English way to swear at someone else. I had chosen 'Fuck Off!' the good old Saxon 'go to' favourite. However, having looked at the vast variety of ways that you can say that same thing in France, I was beginning to wonder why he bothered.

Perhaps the most infamous, due to the ex-French President Sarkozy, is 'Casse-Toi!' Roughly translated to sod/fuck off. In 2008 while being jostled in a large crowd, he reached out to force his way through. One person in the crowd told him not to touch them, to which he replied 'casse-toi alors pauv con!' Which roughly means 'fuck off then you arsehole'. Unfortunately for Sarkozy this was caught clearly on the sound system and kindly transmitted to everyone else in the crowd. At the next election he was booted out!

You can add to this 'fuck off' scenario by exploring the very useful verb 'foutre' meaning 'to do'. Just as 'fuck' can be used in many forms so 'foutre' can be very adaptable. Here are some of the most useful uses:

'Foutre la Merde', meaning 'to fuck up'

'Rien à Foutre', or even 'Je m'en Fous', meaning 'don't give a fuck'

'Ne rien Foutre' meaning 'to do fuck all'

And my personal favourite:

'Aller se Faire Foutre' meaning 'go fuck yourself'.

The other thing to remember with these French 'Gros Mots' is that one expression can be either soft or hard depending how angry the user is. The best example of this is the word 'Dégage' which can stretch from a friendly 'get out of the way' to 'Fuck Off!' depending on just how angry the user actually is.

The final one for you to remember, and practice for that time in the future when some of these expletives are shouted in your direction by an irate French person: 'Ta Gueule', basically 'shut the fuck up!'

Okay, you are now safe to return to my first pétanque training session. After a couple of hours I was exhausted and was somewhat happy to see the Professor, Henri and Maurice stagger off. They were still arguing about the last disputed measurement between piglet and boule.

I am not sure if this match ended because it had actually ended or because I had run out of Ricard! Although looking at their stagger I am not sure that it could possibly have continued for much longer.

There followed many happy occasions where I was instructed on all the finer points of the game by the Professor. This naturally led to me passing on my expertise to whichever guest joined us in France for a break.

Imagine my annoyance when I was usually soundly beaten by these interlopers who had never picked up a boule before, or had even undertaken the extreme training regime offered by the Professor.

However, I was definitely getting better and even managed to introduce some gamesmanship to upset the locals and help me win games. The first was to question the result of a measurement made by anyone for any reason. This measurement being critical to either a win or loss of a point.

This immediately resulted in a reddening of the face and a determined re-measurement of the challenged distance. This was normally followed by at least two other people measuring the same distance with a lot of tutting and shaking of heads. They nearly always screwed up the following shot.

The next winning tactic was to make a subtle farting noise as they concentrated on the shot in hand. Their boule would land metres away from the target as they spun round searching for the offending noise.

Another favourite was to dispute an obvious and I mean obvious winning shot. This always led to an argument between everyone in the two teams and most of the bystanders who had gathered to watch. Again, their following shot was a disaster.

Finally, I found that handing someone my tape measure in inches to measure off a disputed distance caused havoc. They just could not work out what was going on, and were totally confused by the concept of inches. This continued for about 10 minutes during which time they missed everything.

At that time, I desperately searched for a joke stretchable elastic tape measure on the internet but unfortunately never found one!

Their passion was outstanding and everything about this game seemed very important. I guess this must be a Latin thing as I could not imagine the same approach in the UK.

However, the French clearly are a passionate Nation. Arguments explode out of nowhere then die down and disappear just as quickly. Discussions over something as simple as wine quickly degenerate into violent speeches on the pros and cons of Cote de Rhone over Bordeaux. Even their National Anthem 'La Marseillaise' is sung on every occasion with extreme passion by everyone.

But that could be due to the wording I guess, when translated you realise that you could not actually sing it without some passionate feeling. It's not a case of the 'God save our gracious Queen' type of material. Which even the most ardent royalist would have to admit is a song about an unelected head of State rather than a Nation, and a bit dull. Let's have a look at some of the words and compare.

La Marseillaise starts off by telling folks to wake up to the fact that 'tyranny's bloody standard' is raised against them. Then points out that you can hear the 'roar of those ferocious soldiers' as they come to attack. It then continues by casually informing everyone that those soldiers intend 'to cut the throats of your sons and your women'. And that is just the first verse.

We then get to the crux of the whole thing with the chorus which is always sung very loudly and with much aggression. Here it is verbatim.

TO ARMS CITIZENS,

FORM YOUR BATTALIONS,

LET'S MARCH, LET'S MARCH,

LET THEIR IMPURE BLOOD

  WATER OUR FURROWS.

I think you can see my point here, it started with a warning that they are coming to cut your throat. It then follows that up with the French filling the trenches with the blood of their enemies. All very strong stuff.

Meanwhile back in the UK it's 'long to reign over us, God save the Queen' etc. And you have to admit, who actually knows all the words to the UK Anthem. How many times have you watched an international sports event only to see various players mumble 'rhubarb, rhubarb' because they do not know the words? Everyone in France appears to know at least the first two verses, and of course the chorus of 'La Marseillaise'.

(In answer to the obvious question, why is the French National Anthem so bloody? Well it basically started out as a 'rally to arms' song in 1792 after the declaration of war against Austria. Its name coming from being sung in great earnest by volunteers from Marseille as they marched to the capitol.

Like most things in France it has had its ups and downs being replaced once and even being banned outright. It was finally adapted as the French National Anthem in 1879.)

However, hang on a minute. Have you ever looked at the second verse of the UK National Anthem? This is more like it; scattering her enemies, making them all fall and confounding their tricks etc.

Maybe we should ensure that the first two verses are sung instead of the customary first verse; it might increase the fervour. And anyway, at least our royalty has staying power. Elizabeth II seems to go on forever while France's Louis XIX's reign only lasted 20 minutes!

This passion with pétanque also had a financial attraction as I was soon to discover. The tournaments, competitions and events all over the country normally have cash as the prize. They may get a plastic trophy to go with it but believe me it's the cash that is king.

After about six months of my involvement with friendly games in the village and with friends at home, the Professor decided it was time for me to try the real thing. By this he meant a real competition and there was one coming up in Caylus.

His insistence that I join him could have had something to do with his normal playing partner being not available, but I will give him the benefit of the doubt on that one. We arrived, signed in, payed our entrance fee and waited for the competition to start.

It was at this moment, looking around, that I realised that most of these folks had travelled some considerable distance for the competition and were in deadly earnest.

The Professor continually reminded me that all I had to do was just keep throwing boules in the direction of the piglet, he would do the rest. And that's basically how the first round went. I threw my boules in the direction of the piglet and the Professor blasted our opponents' boules out of the park with much venom.

Our opponents seemed angrier that I was English and should not actually be allowed to play this game, rather than losing.

The second and third rounds went much the same way but with stiffer competition; however I could see the professor was tiring. He was actually beginning to miss a few shots, something I had never seen before. And the next round, the quarter finals, was against some previous champions, this was not looking good.

We started off okay with me getting closer to the piglet than before and the Professor keeping up his bombardment. Then they retaliated with some excellent play which put us very close. At this moment the Professor missed a vital shot with his final boule and left me standing there with just one left. "Okay" he casually said, "just throw it hard at their boule near the piglet and we get the point."

Er! what? So, with dozens of hardened pétanque veterans watching, he wanted me to shoot at the offending winning ball and knock it out of play! Well, having had some minor acting experience in the past I thought I could at least play this part. Therefore, I walked up to the circle trying to look as though I knew what I was doing. I threw my boule in the general direction of the opponent's ball as hard as I could, while probably shutting my eyes. It knocked them out of the way winning us the end, and leaving the score at 12-12.

They were so shocked that I had accomplished this completely unexpected hit that they completely went to pieces. The Professor quickly cleaning things up before they could recover. So, we had won the quarter finals, and the Professor was in full professorship mode. This was evident as he annoyed them even more by explaining where they had gone wrong, and that I was just a novice!

Suddenly he stopped, turned and was making his way quickly up to the organiser's tent.

"Where are we going?" I enquired.

"To get our winnings," he responded.

"Winnings, what winnings?" I asked.

"The quarter final winnings," he explained, while looking at me as if I had just asked the most stupid question on the planet.

That got me walking quicker and we both arrived at the tent rubbing our hands together. After a quick rather heated debate between the Professor and the organisers, it became apparent that all was not well. It would appear that a couple of jokers had arrived before us, claimed our prize, been paid out in cash and wandered off.

"Putain!" I said

"Merde Alors!" said the Professor

So that was a bit of a costly team talk the Professor had given our opposition, and with that major disappointment we walked back to the competition. Unfortunately, only to be completely annihilated in the semi-finals!

CHAPTER SIX

The Bar, Loto and the Moles

Driving back from Caylus, while pondering as to who was spending my 50 euro quarter final winnings, I was struck by a few French oddities. First was the amount of folk who had hung their bed linen out of the bedroom window. By this I mean sheets, duvets and maybe even the odd mattress or two. And they didn't always look too clean.

Was this an attempt to freshen the bedding up, a statement about the ownership of such a luxury item or just because that's how it has always been done. I would have thought that, in this modern age of washing machines, this requirement would be redundant. But evidently not, as nearly every house I passed had something valiantly waving out of the window.

The second thing in plain sight for all to see was the number of guys peeing by the roadside. Now, I do not mean discretely tucked away out of sight; I mean stood in the road by the car peeing. This was especially evident if you were on a road with a small layby. These all had a line of guys peeing. They even have a name for it in France, 'Urine Sauvage'. *(Wild peeing!)*

This apparently became a major problem in Paris with the Mayor forming an anti peeing group called 'The Bad behaviour Brigade'. Their job was to give out appropriate fines to offenders; but where we lived everyone did it, and not just in the street. As I walked the dogs one morning, I passed Bernard's house. He was in his front garden peeing, fag in one hand, waving to me with the other, quite impressive really.

On another occasion Francois, the Mayor, had given me a lift to a meeting at the Chasse Federation Headquarters. As he got out of the car he stopped, unzipped, and started to pee in the car park while continuing his conversation to me. Finally, just to prove that this was no sexist scenario, Madeline while walking with the sheep one afternoon, stopped, squatted and did a pee in the middle of the road by our farmhouse. I noted that the collie dog discretely looked the other way!

The other thing that was obvious to me was the number of tourists that descended on this part of France during the warmer months. Yet this fact did not seem to register much on the psyche of the French in their laid back, shut the shop lifestyle. But it certainly registered on us.

Every day walkers would pass through Loser looking red, tired and in need of sustenance. Often, they would stop at our farmhouse and ask for their water bottle to be filled or enquire if there was a bar nearby; there wasn't.

Once, an American lady was so dehydrated, and in need of help, that I gave her a drink of water and offered to run her back to her lodgings in Caylus in my car. She was so relieved that her life had been saved that she rushed into her lodgings and came out with a painting that she had recently completed.

This was presented to me as a gift for, as she had written on the back, 'saving my life!' I laughed and accepted the painting and went home. Some years later this painting re-emerged from a cupboard as I was looking for something else.

I casually looked up the name written on the back using the internet to see if she was a known amateur. She wasn't, she was a well-known professional, in fact a professor at a prestigious American university, whose paintings sell for thousands of dollars! This could have been the most highly recompensed drink of water in history!

You could immediately see an opportunity here, one that was being casually overlooked. So, as usual with anything involving French bureaucracy, we approached the Mayor. Our question was quite simple, what were the possibilities of opening up a bar in Loser to exploit this passing traffic?

His immediate reaction was one of puzzlement, why would anyone want to do that? We explained that this might be a good idea to make some money for the village and he began to see the light.

"How does anyone get a licence to sell drink?" we asked, thinking perhaps a stall in the square.

"We've already got one," he explained, "It's for the Salle de Fête."

(The hall for festivities or the village hall, every village has one; in Loser this was a small hall capable of holding about 60 people.)

"So, the village has a licence to sell drink but doesn't?" we said, "then why has it got a licence?"

"For the village fête run by the Comité de Fêtes," he continued as this was the most obvious thing in the world.

"But this village hasn't had a fête for years and there isn't any Comité," came our rather surprised response.

So here exposed for all to see was the fundamental difference between a Brit and a Frenchman. The Brit immediately sees an opportunity to make a buck, the Frenchman immediately sees something that might take work and keep him away from lunch.

It really didn't take much imagination to see that by offering something at the weekends, the village could make money. Especially as we were surrounded by other small villages that, like Loser, were completely dead at the weekend.

However, the Mayor was warming to this idea, if we were willing to open something up on Saturday and Sunday afternoons, he would fund the purchase of the initial stock. He would do this from the Mairie petty cash if we would repay the costs at some stage. It was quite clear that he didn't expect ever to get anything back, and that this would fall flat quite quickly. He was wrong.

We popped a note out to all the villagers that the bar would be open at the Salle des Fêtes on Saturday. We put out some signs on the road to capture passing traffic and of course we spread the word wherever we went.

That first weekend proved a big success, in fact we had a job closing each day as pétanque games raged and villagers gossiped. Within two months we had paid back the Mayor and handed over the same again in profit. He was speechless.

One of the main beneficiaries of the bar was the old folks who lived in the village. *(By this I actually mean most of the people who lived in the village!)* They suddenly started to receive a very nice basket of food and wine as a Christmas gift.

But this is France so even with a free gift nothing goes to plan. The first hiccup was our intention to invite all the eligible oldies to the Salle des Fêtes for an 'apero', and to collect their hamper.

What we didn't realise was that certain families in this small village did not speak to each other; this for reasons long forgotten. Plus, to make matters worse it wasn't just the not talking, they also avoided each other at all costs. So, the Mayor asked if we would deliver the hampers by hand instead.

This seemed to go against the whole idea of bringing the village together thus we said no. And, as it was us who were funding the event, he reluctantly agreed.

(For a guy who was a senior army officer he always seemed very reluctant to be involved in conflict, never could understand that.)

So, the invitations went out and there we sat with the Professor dressed as Santa waiting to see what would happen. *(Incredibly the Professor had a fake white beard over his.... well, over his white beard!)* Meanwhile the Mayor paced up and down with a speech written on several pieces of paper. He clearly wasn't going to miss a potential 'vote for me' opportunity with the Mayoral elections approaching.

Slowly the families started to turn up, including several that the Mayor had told us would never attend such an occasion. There was one old couple who had not been seen for some time and had a grudge against a few other families in the village. An audible gasp went through the hall as they sauntered in, sat down and offered 'bonsoirs' to the surrounding folk. Including, I might add, a family who they had avoided for about 30 years!

To this day I do not know if it was the free hamper, curiosity or just that this was the first invite they had received for years. But, turn up they did, and everyone seemed to enjoy the occasion. It did leave a few old folks though who were unable to come due to ill health. Therefore, we did do some deliveries after all.

One of these was an old guy in his eighties, Lucien, who was pretty much immobile but still had a very sharp brain. He shocked us by suddenly breaking out into English and without much prompting told us his story.

He was born in Algeria, which up to 1962 was a French colony, thus he had always thought of himself as French. Therefore, although he was very young, he was quick to make his way to France to join up and fight against the Germans at the start of the Second World War. He did succeed in joining the French forces but only in time to find himself on a transport ship bound for England. Once there, he joined a volunteer group of 'Free French' army personnel who moved to the midlands to train with the RAF as bomber crew.

He ended up as a rear gunner in a Halifax bomber and was a very proud member of the RAF. Unfortunately, this was short lived as Charles de Gaulle *(probably in between assassination attempts)* had the Free French fighters all moved to a French only squadron.

Thus, Lucien could no longer claim to be in the RAF. He had many hair-raising stories to tell and tell them he did...often. Every time I saw him, I had to listen to the same stories, he never tired of telling them.

I was beginning to question the validity of some of these tales then one day he pulled out an old RAF canvas bag. Inside the bag were the remnants of a uniform, some very impressive medals and best of all, photos.

Photos of him as a very young man sat on a Halifax wing, in the cockpit, in the rear gun emplacement and generally larking about with a small group of RAF chaps.

After the war, during which he was wounded during a flight, he found his way back to France and ended up in Loser. Incredibly when he went to the 'Préfecture' *(Basically the main centre of administration for a region)* to claim his French identity card, it was refused. Without it he would not be able to get a job, so this was a big deal. At that time, it was not straightforward for someone from Algeria to prove French citizenship.

So, to recap, when France was attacked by Germany, he had rushed to defend France, willingly been shipped to continue that fight from England, been trained in one of the most dangerous jobs in bomber command, been wounded and made his way back. Only to be refused an identity card!

At that time the Mayor of Loser was a certain Monsieur Bosse, remember that name? That was the family who once owned our farmhouse; and we had bumped into one of his descendants earlier. Monsieur Bosse was quite an important chap as he had been one of the leading figures in the local 'Marquis.' *(The small groups who made up the French resistance during the war; we will cover some of their history later.)*

On hearing Lucien's story, he drove him straight back to the 'Préfecture'. He rushed Lucien in and had an amazing row. First with the unfortunate clerk who had refused Lucien's identity card, then the 'Sous Préfet' *(the sub-Prefect, this being the French State's representative in the region)* and finally with the 'Préfet' himself.

He demanded to know why someone who had fought through the whole war for France, while they had been sitting on their arses, didn't qualify for an identity card!

This was clearly not an argument that had much mileage, especially if you actually want to draw breath the next day. So out walked Lucien with his identity card, and his new life in France.

One other story that had a personal element was when Lucien told me that he was in fact not the first RAF chap in the village. This was a bit of a bombshell *(sorry about that)* as nobody had

163

mentioned anything about any other RAF involvement in Loser.

Apparently during the war years our farmhouse was unused and derelict. In fact, it was only used by a few animals for shelter and local children to play in. One night during the war a lorry pulled up outside Monsieur Bosse's house and deposited a slightly dishevelled RAF pilot. He had been shot down somewhere in Northern France. This was about the 4th drop off point for this pilot on his route south to his escape across the Pyrenees to Spain.

Our farmhouse was the obvious hiding place, and he stayed there in secret for a few days before being shuttled off again to Toulouse for his final leg home. I don't know if he made it; I hope he did. And you have to remember this; if Monsieur Bosse or anyone else involved had been caught, they would have been shot! Makes you think doesn't it.

Years later Lucien passed away, the last of the few. And I have to say that the Mayor did a great job in ensuring that a fitting funeral was arranged. As we lowered Lucien into his tomb, I said farewell to Tail-End Charlie, and the last I saw was a glint of sun bouncing off the row of medals that were attached to the lid of his coffin. Next to them was a cloth RAF Air Gunner badge that he had never mentioned, and I had never seen before!

So, the villagers had their hampers and even a few who were in hospital received something, and everyone was well pleased. Well this is France, not everyone.

Madame Vay apparently threw her hamper into the village 'poubelle' *(rubbish bin)* as soon as she found out that the leather coated Gestapo bloke had something to do with it!

As I have touched on the subject it is perhaps worth a few words on the 'Marquis' during the war. Lucien explained much about this group of resistant fighters that I had just not understood before.

At the beginning of the German occupation the French Resistance groups were mostly communist groups who were against right wing politics, in particular Fascists; thus, contra both Germans and the French Vichy government.

They were not particularly active at first and were a small minority. The vast majority of French folk just muddled through making the most of the situation. I would imagine with many Gallic shrugs.

However, when Hitler invaded Russia, a compulsory work order was issued to all men of military age in France by the Germans. Suddenly the Marquis were gaining recruits from every background. But they lacked training and, more importantly, weapons.

These shortfalls were filled by weapon drops from England and by British SOE *(Special Operations Executive)* personnel parachuting in to help train the recruits in guerrilla warfare and sabotage.

In truth there was much internal division amongst the Marquis groups; perhaps exacerbated by their communist ideals versus Charles de Gaulle's anti-communist HQ in London. However, finally in May 1943 all the Marquis groups came together under one banner. This under the leadership of one Jean Moulin. They ultimately became the French Forces of the Interior *(FFI)* numbering some 100,000 fighters.

These brave folks risked being shot if discovered as they tried to bring chaos to the German military infrastructure. In fact, their activities had some disastrous setbacks including many reprisals. Perhaps the most infamous being the village of Oradour-sur-Glane. Here 642 men, women and children were massacred by the

German Waffen SS as they completely destroyed the village.

This was supposedly in retaliation to the capture of an SS officer by the local Marquis. After the war this village was left empty in its destroyed state as a permanent memorial to those who were murdered.

Interestingly, the SS had been tipped off by another group who I had never heard of; the Milice. These were a French collaborator paramilitary force controlled by the right-wing French Vichy government.

They were much feared and hated as they worked alongside the Gestapo to help fight against the French Resistance. They were known for being brutal with executions, torture and assassinations being normal behaviour. They also helped in the rounding up of Jewish people and resistance supporters for deportation.

Perhaps the greatest achievement of the Marquis groups was the invaluable help given to the allies both before, during and after D-Day. Without them the invasion would have been much tougher and cost many more lives.

Before the war ended Jean Moulin was exposed by someone, captured, tortured and died after a suicide attempt. To this day it is not known who betrayed him. During the war many French resistance members were betrayed and killed. It is a sobering thought that it was probably another French person who had betrayed them.

As to the Milice, well their numbers had reached some 30,000 by the end of the war, and after the Normandy landings those who did not flee to Germany were doomed. Generally, they were imprisoned for treason or executed, sometimes in large numbers, on the spot.

As to the memory of the resistance fighters, well, as you travel through France today you will see their story displayed. There are countless plaques on the walls of French villages stating that a resistance fighter or group of fighters were murdered at this location. Their fight has not been forgotten by the older generation either.

Once while walking our dogs in Caylus a very old chap walked up and asked what breed our dogs were. I explained to him that they were Schnauzers, a breed not often seen in France. I also told him that the breed came from Germany.

"Are you German?" he rather aggressively asked.

"Er! no I'm English," I responded, not actually knowing if this answer was good or bad news.

He stepped up closer into my space and said, "GERMANS PAH!" while slicing his finger across his throat.

With that he sauntered off mumbling something about the war, leaving myself and the dogs all looking at each other bewildered!

Thus, our endeavours to bring the village to life had been a great success. The bar continued for many years funding gifts for the old folks, buying various pieces of equipment for the village and in particular purchasing a large number of tables with bench seating.

There were enough for the whole village to sit down together for a meal. Many happy days were spent watching the village come together, and once again having somewhere to meet up, play cards, play pétanque or just share a beer.

After all this had been achieved, and the years had rolled by, we eventually decided that it was time to hand over the running of the bar to the French villagers. It would be nice to get our weekends back as, although some village members gave a hand with the running of the bar, mostly it was us who did the graft.

This handover was successfully accomplished, and we left them to it. After about 24 months and many arguments later the bar had shut!

169

About the same time as we had opened the bar, we tackled the issue of the missing Comité des Fêtes. It seemed crazy that a village had no formal function to attend, especially so as this yearly fête is very much a French tradition. So, we asked someone who had voiced the same opinion if he would be the chairman of a proposed new Comité.

His name was Louis and he was keen. He was the sort of guy who always looked as though he had too much energy as he rushed from one place to another. Generally having the right intensions but rarely hitting the back of the net, you probably know someone like this. He had the annoying habit of agreeing to everything you said, then doing something completely different. However, any port in a storm.

After some arm twisting, we were able to put together enough folks from the village to form the Comité, and following a quick voting-in process we were in business.

However, this is France, nothing is that easy, we had no money. The previous Comité had left nothing. There was no stock except hundreds of useless soup bowls that a previous Comité member had thought was a good idea to purchase. Even the donkey's head had gone walkies.

It is apparently normal for an incoming new Comité to inherit funds, drink, tables and chairs. Plus, various other accoutrements that make up the successful running of a village event. We had nothing, and in true French fashion the answer to this conundrum was not easy to find.

"How do you normally fund a fête?" we asked Louis.

"Easy," he replied, "you just use the profit made from ticket sales from the last fête."

"But there hasn't been a last fête," we pointed out.

"Yes, er! then we just use the money from the ticket sales for the next fête," he suggested.

"So, we hire a band, buy loads of food and wine for the village meal, rent a massive marquee, rent a beer tent and a wooden dance floor, all in the hope that we sell some tickets?" we enquired.

The blank look on the faces of the new Comité demonstrated that they were quickly cottoning on to the depth of the problem they had taken on. No wonder we all were quickly voted in by the rest of the villagers; well, those who bothered to turn up to the meeting.

But hang on, we had a Salle des Fêtes with its own kitchen free of charge, and we had the bar nicely positioned inside. It was not big enough for a full village function but was surely big enough to run some money-making events.

"Is there nothing else that previous Comités have done to make money?" we asked.

"Only the Loto," Louis explained, "that is always very popular with folks from other villages, but we have no money for prizes!"

(In France a Loto is exactly the same as our game Bingo. However, without the amusing 'two little ducks' or 'legs eleven'! Prizes can range from electrical items to joints of meat, but the main prize is nearly always a large cash sum.)

"Okay, what about running some themed meals in the Salle des Fêtes and using the profits for Loto prizes?" we ventured.

At this stage in true French fashion our new Comité burst into a heated debate about how this would be a difficult, would never work and still posed the problem of potential lack of support.

However, we managed to persuade them that one disastrous meal would not be as bad as being in debt to thousands of euros due to a fête disaster. So, we had a plan, all we had to do was stick to it; but this is France!

The meals worked fine, and we quickly put together enough profit to start buying some Loto prizes. However, it was very hard to explain to our French colleagues the tactic of using sales and special offers to fill our prize list. We would shoot off to a shop that was displaying perhaps a toaster for half price, snap it up, and put it in the prize pile. The next time we looked at the pile something else would be attached to the toaster to bring it up to the full original price.

They simply could not understand our logic of buying something when it was cheap or on special offer. To them it had to be the full price else they were cheating the players.

"But its true value is still the full price," we would explain, "It's just that we happen to have got it cheaper."

"But we didn't pay the full price," they would say.

"I know, THAT'S THE POINT," we would gently point out. "This is all about us making profit to run the fête."

It was like treading treacle, but we did eventually put together enough good prizes to run a Loto. What was even better was the facility in a neighbouring village that had a large hall for hire, a professional looking Loto machine, plus a huge screen that simulated the numbers called. What could possibly go wrong?

The first hurdle was the tombola idea.

(In France a tombola is what we would call a raffle in the UK. Tickets sold for a particular prize with the winning ticket pulled some time during the event.)

We fancied that a tombola would add to the coffers and all it needed was one or two good prizes. All we had to do was hard-sell tickets as folks came through the door. "What if nobody buys them?" they all said. "No one sells tombola tickets at a Loto," they continued. And thus, all we got was a mass of reasons why we should not have a tombola. We persevered and explained several times just how easy it is to run and thankfully they finally relented.

The next hurdle was the promotion of the event. Our Comité friends were convinced that you never needed to run a promotion campaign as "everyone knew, didn't they?" We, on the other hand, simply asked "How?" They couldn't answer that of course. They seemed to accept that the rule that governed that everyone knows everyone's business in the village of Loser, equally applied to Loto games.

Too much of a risk for us, so we had some posters and handbills made. Posters were stuck up around the area, and the handbills pushed under people's windscreen wipers at all the local markets. *(I bet you always wondered who did that!)* So, on the chosen night we got to the hall, set up dozens of tables and hundreds of chairs, tested the machine, manned the coffee and cake table, prepared the tombola tickets, peopled the entrance ticket table and .... waited.

If this didn't pay off, we had a big rental bill to pay for the hall, a huge pile of prizes with nowhere to go and a lot of hard work up in smoke. Louis was not fazed, he just rushed about the hall straightening chairs, counting prizes and generally looking very busy.

The rest of the Comité, along with a few valiant helpers from the village, seemed to be slowly edging towards the cake table. The cakes were looking better by the minute having been donated by some of the best cooks in the village. I, on the other hand, was looking out of the window, *(anyone who has read my book 'Please Wipe Your Boots' will realise that I had been extensively trained to do this!)* and it was not good news, it was snowing!

175

Just to add to the misery a thought had suddenly struck me. What happens if two people shout 'Bingo,' 'House,' or as I was soon to find out 'Quine' at the same time? Louis had a simple answer to this.

"We let them pull a number out of the special 'Double Quine' bag and the highest number wins," he said. "Plus," he continued, "the loser gets a bottle of wine."

This was news to us.

"What wine?" we casually enquired.

"Er, the 6 bottles of wine that we brought along as extra prizes," he explained, while looking a bit sheepish. In truth he was going to add them to one of our 'special deal' purchased prizes!

So, there we were at the start of an evening of Loto with 18 nice prizes to give out and a fall-back of 6 bottles of wine in case of double shouts. When I say nice prizes, they were. During the build-up to the event some of the kind folks of Loser had donated money, gifts and best of all boxes of meat products from the local butcher. If only we had some players, that would have been nice.

The event was due to start at 21.00, and by 20.30 with snow still falling outside we had about 30 people in the hall. We needed about 100 to break even so things were looking very grim indeed. Even Louis was seen to have a bead of perspiration on his forehead as he busily lined up a few more perfectly straight tables.

The Mayor was also busy turning all the tombola tickets up the same way and arranging the Loto cards in nice military lines. Even the Professor was hard at work switching on the mid-break coffee urn so that by the mid-break the coffee would be stewed and lukewarm.

Then they started to arrive. A trickle at first, then a rush, then a panicked push to get into the hall in time. It was all hands to the entrance table to cope with the incoming players. And mad mayhem as they fingered the Loto cards that the Mayor had nicely laid out for their perusal.

It would appear that in France it is not good enough just to pick up your Loto playing card, pay your entrance fee and go and sit down. Each card has to be examined and turned over. They then were held up to the light, tutted at, thrown down in a heap and another picked up to start the process over again. Meanwhile a backlog of eager players were queueing up outside in the snow. When I say queueing, what I meant was milling about with a bit of pushing and shoving!

177

We had laid out the hall for a hopeful 200 players, but this was quickly filling so more tables and chairs were sought from the storage room. Quickly every space was being filled, even the stage behind the Loto machine was filling up. As to the tombola, money was being handed over quicker than we could cope with as people jostled to get a ticket. Luckily, we had bought enough tombola tickets to last for several years, we ended up with none left.

So, with every seat taken, every tombola ticket sold, every Loto card picked up and discarded at least 4 times, plus the mid-break coffee gently stewing in the background, we were ready.

Louis was the number caller and my job was to pull the ball out of the machine for his perusal. This should be easy, but we were Loto virgins in a hall of hardened French Loto fanatics. It was an unnerving experience.

We were either calling the numbers too fast or too slow; then Louis would click up the wrong number on the overhead screen or miss a 'QUINE!' shout from the back of the hall. Each of these 'faux Pas' were met by an audible 'Tut' or 'Zut' from our guests, and these quickly turned into a few 'Putains' and 'Merdes' as the evening wore on.

I, for one, was relieved when the mid-break was announced, and everyone rushed up to the coffee and cake table to devour the best cakes and grimace at the coffee that had now been brewing for 2 hours. Many of these players also rushed up to the Loto card table to change their cards.

So, if you had not won anything on your chosen card by the mid-break point, you simply changed it for a different one. I couldn't see the logic in this myself but there they were holding up cards and discarding them again in an urgent need to find that lucky card.

I felt a bit sorry for the Mayor as he had spent about half an hour tidying these cards up again while carefully noting down every Loto number that was called. What on earth he was going to do with that information I will never know.

I noticed at this stage that 4 of our double-call wine bottles had been given out. That left two with nothing else to pacify a double 'Quine' call. I decided not to worry Louis with that one as he already looked as though he had just run two marathons!

After calling out the winning tombola numbers amid much shaking of heads and 'Zuts' we kicked off again. The second half went very much as the first with many more 'Zuts' and

'Putains.' I am not sure if these were being aimed at us or their own bad luck, but by this stage I didn't care.

What worried me more was when we handed over the last bottle of wine to a double 'Quine' caller. I looked at Louis and was greeted by, okay you have guessed by now, a perfectly performed Gallic shrug. The Gods must have been looking down on us that evening. And decided that we had had enough aggravation, as there were no more double calls.

Now, with the last prize given out, there was a mad rush to get out of the hall and get home in the thickening snow. I will always remember the sight of the last player as he pushed out of the doors with half a pig dangling over his shoulder. This was his prize from a winning call!

We were left standing in a daze surrounded by dozens of debris laden tables, overturned chairs, a floor covered in tombola tickets and sweet wrappers, plus the Mayor's carefully arranged Loto cards laying strewn everywhere. All the cake had gone but there was some of the Professor's coffee left!

It was now past midnight. We had been there hours before the start to set everything up. We had worked valiantly for hours during the event to keep it on track, and were now faced with hours to tidy everything up again.

I thought for a moment to call a Strike Action to rally everyone to get behind the task, but no need. At certain times the French can be a stoic lot and they just got on with the task without question. A careful count of the nights takings was eagerly watched by everyone as piles of cash were counted then checked.

The Mayor looked crestfallen as each note was pushed into the growing pile at varying positions, upside down, reverse faced, or even right way up front facing. He would have given anything to get his hands on them to straighten them out, but we didn't have the time.

With much relief and big grins all round we had made a massive profit, more than enough to fund most of a good village fête. All we had to do was agree what type of event we would run and plan it. What could possibly go wrong?

The next day I awoke to a bright, crisp, cold morning, still with the taste of the Professor's coffee lingering in my mouth. I yawned and looked out across my mole hill strewn lawn. What? How? Where the hell did they come from? were my immediate thoughts. I even demonstrated my grasp of the French language by breaking into a nice mixture of English and French swear words.

Now let's be clear here, when I say lawn what I actually mean is grass or maybe, if I am honest, a mixture of moss and grass. But these were uninvited guests and must be dealt with.

A trip to the 'quincaillerie' in Caylus provided an insight into this new mole hill challenge. There were traps, gasses, exploding bombs, poison, sonic sounders and even a device that shot a 9mm blank cartridge into the offending hole.

Now having two dogs of the 'I will eat anything' variety, the poison seemed out of the question. So, I tried a trap, some bombs and a sonic sounder. Out I walked with two carrier bags filled with mole destruction equipment.

Back at the farmhouse as I was burying the sonic sounder, the bombs and the trap in various places on the grass, Henri wandered by. When I say wandered by, I think that Brigette had sent him out to see what I was doing!

Here was a seasoned gardener with much experience, therefore I went over to ask his advice.

"11.00 in the morning and 4.30 in the afternoon," he said, "just be quiet and wait with a shotgun and up they will come."

Now as an ex-clay pigeon shooter I had a shotgun, but was a bit uneasy about firing it into the ground a few metres from my feet. So, I asked him to explain. He convinced me that moles always surface at the same time every day, so I should try it.

Now, in the UK I would have immediately suspecting a wind up, but the French do not have much of a sense of humour and Henri had none, so I gave it a try. After all, it would explain why so many shots could be heard from his garden during the day; they couldn't all be at birds stealing his produce.

I stood there at 11.00 then again in the afternoon with no result. What on earth folks who passed by the farmhouse thought I was doing I will never know. They probably just thought it was some mad English ritual. To make matters worse the sonic sounder was not deterring the moles, the exploding bombs seemed to be encouraging the moles even more and the trap trapped nothing.

The garden was becoming one big mole haven, and nothing seemed to work. The next sound advice came from Jean-Pierre as he walked his sheep and noticed me standing there like a scarecrow armed with a shotgun. He pointed over to my aging tractor, which had been bought more as an ornament rather than to actually do anything.

"G..G..Gas," he said, while pointing at the exhaust pipe. "Gr..Gr..Pipe, gas," he continued to explain.

This guy was not as daft as he looked. If I connected a pipe to the exhaust of the tractor and poked the other end down one of the interconnecting mole holes, the carbon monoxide would do the rest.

So that afternoon I could be seen revving the tractor engine in our garden, with a pipe leaving the exhaust leading into a mole hole in the ground. Smoke could be seen appearing from about a dozen places across the lawn and the smell could be noticed from about 100 metres away.

Several people drove by the house, slowed down, looked completely bewildered and drove off again. Finally, Ollie appeared and stopped to enquire if I was feeling alright. I explained my dilemma and he simply shook his head and said "diesel."

"All you have to do is put a few drops of diesel down each hole," he explained, "the moles hate the smell and will move away."

"Won't they just come back?" I asked.

"No, they will move off quickly into a neighbouring field," he said.

As he said that, we both looked across to Henri's garden which happened to be my neighbouring field. "Voila," he said!

All is fair in love and war so diesel it was going to be. For days I poured diesel into each mound as it appeared and also gassed them with the tractor. The result was always the same, a few days respite then a return of the mole hills in another spot.

Meanwhile I had used all the mole bombs, tried the trap in multiple places and shifted the sonic sounder up and down the garden a dozen times. I had grown tired of looking like an armed scarecrow, and I even ventured back to the 'Quincaillerie' to buy the 9mm firing device.

As I entered the shop the owner nodded sagely as if to confirm that I would definitely be back. He obviously thought that I should have bought this along with all the other dubious deterrents he had already sold me.

185

So just to recap, I had bombed them, stalked them with a shotgun, gassed them, drowned them in diesel, blasted them with sonic beams, tried to trap them and was now endeavouring to shoot them with a touch sensitive 9mm blast.... That never worked either. These putain French moles were something else!

So, in the end I had tried everything, used gallons of diesel fuel, packets of mole bombs and spent hours on other pointless deterrents and was getting nowhere. In fact, I was becoming concerned that if someone wandered into the garden and lit up a cigarette the whole of Loser would go up in flames. I could just see the newspaper headline. 'Brit Blows Up French Village!'

It was another bright, crisp and cold morning as I rose to go and kick over today's offending mole hills. There was one particularly big one right in the centre of the lawn; almost like a statement from the moles...you will never win.

As I prepared to kick the raised soil as far as I could, I noticed a glint on the top of the mound. Closer inspection revealed a ring nicely placed at the very top. Not just any ring, a solid gold ring. This was evident just by looking, it had come out of the earth looking as though it had just been polished.

It was of an ancient design that I had never seen before. And had no marks other than a very small indistinguishable punch mark of some sort on the inside.

I took this to be a truce by the moles, perhaps a peace offering. Or was it that one of the moles, while burrowing through the ground, had this ring stuck on his pointy nose? The only way to remove it was by surfacing to the top of the mound, then back-peddling.

Who knows? One thing is for sure. I never tried to gas them again and every mound that appeared after that day was closely inspected for potential treasure before simply being flattened by my boot.

Knowing what bureaucracy is like in France I did check with the Mayor as to what I should do with the ring. This was after having it tested and confirming that it was indeed 24 carat gold. He simply shrugged and said that it did not constitute treasure trove as its value was minimal and was simply a lost personal item. In other words, keep it. Advice that I willingly accepted.

I have never seen a ring like it since and have to reflect that, being probably hundreds of years old, it must have been a big loss for someone. This area has been rural farmland for centuries and farmers in the past simply could not have afforded such a thing.

My only guess is that the path next to the farmhouse once was used by folk on horseback and this small sized ring was lost while passing by. So, the moral of this story is, always have a look at the top of any mole hill before you kick it to destruction; you never know.

CHAPTER SEVEN

The Vendange & the Chasse Exam

In France it is not unusual for items to suddenly appear on your terrace without any explanation. I've already mentioned the 'neighbour's day' flowers and the various garden products from Henri, but this morning it was a 5-litre plastic can. Inside was some red liquid, no label, no note just a plastic container filled with red....stuff.

A quick sniff test revealed the smell of wine. The following taste test first turned my face inside out, then made my toes curl up and finally made the hair on my head stand up straight. This could only be one thing of course, this was my payment for helping Jean-Pierre with the Vendange. It also explained why Madeline's hair always looked as though it was stood up on end!

The Vendange in France is very much a tradition unchanged for centuries, it is the harvest of grapes for wine making. In a world of modern machinery many of the major wine producers still harvest by hand. Thus, with about 750,000 hectares to harvest, and with about 3,000 different types of grape grown, they need an army of grape pickers. In fact, it is estimated that some 100,000 jobs are filled by temporary workers during this harvest time. Some taking on the picking role 'coupeur' and others to carry baskets 'porteur'.

Jean-Pierre was not in this major league of course, he just had a small vineyard of about a few acres. However, come the harvest he always needed a hand and it was a village tradition to muck in. As he wandered by one day he had shouted out,

"Vendange...vendange, Samedi...Samedi."

I did not have a clue what he was saying so in my usual modus operandi when confronted with undecipherable French, I put up my thumbs and shouted "Oui." Later that afternoon the Mayor stopped by the gate and asked if it was true that I was helping with the Vendange on Saturday. My blank look explained everything, and he carefully outlined what I had actually volunteered for. I was going to be a 'coupeur'.

During that afternoon's pétanque lesson the Professor also let it drop that he was helping on Saturday. He then casually asked if I was staying for the traditional post Vendange lunch. Again, not really knowing what I was doing, I said yes, of course. The Professor's puzzled look and slight smile should have been a warning, but it went over my head.

On the way back from his day of sheep tending Jean-Pierre made eating signs with his hands, to which I again responded with "Oui." I followed this as usual with a quick thumbs up, he seemed well pleased. Thus, the die was cast, my fate was sealed, and I was heading for yet another strange French experience.

It was testament to just how much land made up Jean-Pierre's farm that I had no idea where his vineyard was. Therefore, I simply headed off to his farmhouse on the Saturday in question completely clueless; in more ways than one.

There was one blessing that morning though, the incredibly irritating continual shotgun sounding blasts had stopped. Emanating from some mechanical device, they had been making a racket for a couple of weeks, every couple of minutes...bang!

As a newcomer to the village I didn't want to complain as no one else seemed to notice it. But I noticed it, and this particular morning its absence was a big relief. As I arrived at Jean-Pierre's farmhouse I was met by much activity, he had family in attendance who had arrived to help. It was a bit of a shock, after knowing Jean-Pierre and Madeline, that the family members all looked ...well... normal.

I was pointed in the right direction across an adjacent field and set off. Unfortunately leaving behind the first signs of tension as both Madeline and Jean-Pierre's sister had jostled to be the guiding finger. The vineyard quickly came into sight along with the happy helpers. Bernard, the Mayor, the Professor, Henri and a few of Jean-Pierre family members were already busy cutting bunches of grapes from the vines.

Meanwhile Jean-Pierre himself was walking up and down with a huge basket on his head collecting the grapes. This he walked continually to empty into a massive barrel sat on the back of his old wooden trailer. Balanced precariously on top of the barrel was some kind of mincer, and valiantly turning the handle was his brother in law.

Thus, I joined this happy production line as we attacked the rows of red grapes and minced them into the barrel.

As you do, I tasted some of the grapes and now you know how I had quickly recognised the provenance of the gifted wine. They were 'piqué' *(sharp or sour)* and totally inedible. Was he really going to make wine with this stuff? I asked the Professor if he had ever tasted any of Jean-Pierre's vintage offering, he confirmed my suspicions by a shocked shake of the head.

"He always gives me some, but I pour it down the drain," he explained, "I won't do it this year though as I think it screwed up my Fosse Septic!"

As I was trying to work out if we could sell it as an industrial cleaner, I noticed a big chunk of machinery wired up to two large tractor batteries. On closer inspection it was an air pressure machine that could be set up to make a large bang at intervals. The purpose being to scare off animals or birds from whatever produce it was defending. In this case it was there, apparently, to stop 'Sangliers' *(wild boar)* from eating the grapes.

On closer inspection there was a setting on the side that would create the noise from once every 4 hours all the way down to every 2 minutes. It was set at two minutes! So, Jean-Pierre was the culprit, I should have guessed. Henri saw me looking and told me not to worry as he was going to 'adjust' it before next year. I never heard it again.

With all the grapes gathered and a second barrel nearly full of crushed red stuff, we all set off back to Jean-Pierre's farmhouse for an 'apero.'

Plus, what I thought was going to be the traditional Vendange meal.

Actually entering the farmhouse itself it was a bit like walking back in time, heavy dark wood furniture, a huge soot stained fireplace and a large number of sticky fly papers hanging from the ceiling. Each heavily adorned with dead flies, fascinating.

In one corner sat the Matriarch of the family, Jean-Pierre's mother. A very large lady and pretty much immobile, she still lived at the farmhouse along with himself and Madeline. She was clearly in charge of the household and their lives, and to be honest was a bit unnerving.

No wonder Jean-Pierre was terrified of her. She sat watching everyone very carefully, especially me. I was closely examined like some specimen in a zoo. She obviously had never seen an English bloke before and was quite bemused.

It would appear that poor Madeline spent most of her time as his mother's carer, this along with the full range of tough farm jobs. It was no surprise when I heard later that shortly after they had got married she had run away. She was eventually found hiding in a pig sty and returned to the household never to escape again!

There was an old range cooker to one side and as we all sipped our Ricard apero, Madeline and Jean-Pierre's sister continued their jostling. They were each trying to take control of the cooking process. Much was being made of the chicken as they heatedly discussed whether it was ready or not, each time both glancing back at me. I was beginning to wonder if I was on the menu as well!

Well the vast old farmhouse table was being set up so this was a signal for the Mayor and Henri to bid their farewells and leave. This was a bit of a shock, I thought we were all staying for the lunch. Then, to my horror, both Bernard and the Professor got up to leave.

"Er..aren't you staying for the meal?" I pleaded.

"No, no we're off now," said the Professor, "good luck," he added as they quickly disappeared through the door smiling.

So, there I sat, all alone with Jean-Pierre's family all looking at me. Now if I could speak French, I could have probably come up with a great excuse to leave as well, but I didn't. And I had clearly signalled that I was here for the meal, so I was stuck.

The first course was being served up, so we all went to the table, the Matriarch at one end and me at the other. She clearly wanted to keep an eye on me. This course was a bowl of soup and gently floating on the top of this traditional fare was spaghetti.

Now at this stage I will remind you that Jean-Pierre and Madeline were almost illiterate thus it was somewhat of a surprise to discover that the aforementioned spaghetti was 'alphabetti spaghetti!' I pointed to the soup and laughed; no one else did so that fell flat. Meanwhile I noticed a bit of pushing and shoving around the cooker as Madeline and the sister tried to gain control.

Trying hard to say something I turned to Jean-Pierre as he poured out undrinkable wine to his guests.

"Er..chicken," I pointed, "a vendange tradition?" I asked.

"No just for you," he indicated, while pulling his finger across his throat!

So that was comforting, the poor chicken had been dragged out of the coop and bumped off just because I was staying for the meal. The chicken was deposited on the table and the Matriarch signalled for Jean-Pierre to carve.

This he did by extracting his very sharp, over large pocket knife from his trouser pocket. He snapped it open and began carving. I tried not to think of what else had been cut with this knife or what else had been in his pocket; better not to know.

Again, everyone was looking at me and it was obvious that I was expected to take the first piece. Normally I would be polite and just take anything but on this occasion I took a slice of the breast. This was basically because the chicken looked undercooked to me and still retained its feet, head and various other parts that would never normally reach the table. In fact, with a bit of medical care I think it could have got up and walked off by itself!

My selection caused some smiles and a nodding of heads. This English bloke was polite, he just took the worst piece of the chicken. I noted with some horror that the feet and the head were finding their way onto the plates and were being eaten with gusto. This main meal broke the ice a bit and they started to chat with each other, I was no longer a novelty.

They even tried their best to include me in the conversation, and soon my head was hurting from trying hard to translate the bullet fast French. Every time I looked blank at a question it was just repeated at twice the decibels. They either assumed that I was deaf or that increasing the volume performed some magical translation on the French language. Meanwhile out of the corner of my eye I saw the Matriarch continue her staring.

One thing that I found odd was the large amount of bread used throughout this meal. A large pile had been deposited on the table since the start but no bread plates. It was simply torn to bits by the guests and eaten, dipped, waved about as they talked, all the time leaving a pile of debris on the table.

I also noticed that I was the only one not drinking the wine. I got around this difficulty by miming driving a car each time more was offered.

After some strange looking cake and a small cup of treacle thick black coffee I decided it was time to make my escape. A bit of yawning and several glances at my watch did the trick. And after rushing through the obligatory hand shaking and 'la bise' I rushed away. They were probably as relieved as me, and glancing back I noticed that each window had a face watching me go.

I never repeated this experience as, after Henri's adjustments to the sanglier repellent, Jean-Pierre's grapes never survived in sufficient quantity to warrant another Vendange. You could tell which of the sangliers had eaten the most grapes of course, they were the ones with their fur standing on end!

As for my so called Vendange friends, well they all laughed when I told of my dining experience. They added of course that they had all tried this once themselves, but never again. My enquiry as to why on earth they hadn't warned me was met by "we thought you would enjoy something typically French!" Thanks!

One of the things that we quickly discovered on moving to France was that we had brought too much stuff with us. The farmhouse quickly filled with it, every spare storage location was filled with it and even a lean-to at the back was filled to the roof. Something had to be done. In our defence, we had no idea where we were going or what we would need, thus we had put everything into storage. The size of the removal lorry with its huge trailer should have been a clue.

Now there are two excellent ways to get rid of unwanted stuff in France. The first is the very popular 'Vide-Grenier.'

(Empty attic, the French equivalent to the UK car boot sale.)

The second is the equally popular 'Vide-Maison.'

(Empty house, this being an opportunity to advertise that you have a quantity of stuff at your house for sale.)

Here though is another example of the strange approach that the French have to anything of a commercial nature. They set up and attend Vide-Greniers in large numbers, but they just do not seem to want to sell anything. The prices they ask are astronomical, finding the owner of a stall is a challenge and if you arrive between 12.00 and 15.00, they have covered over their stall and are busy with lunch.

If you make a sensible offer for anything on their stall they look at you in complete horror as if you had insulted them in some way. However, I noted that if the same person wanted to buy something, they wanted it for nothing!

The other thing very noticeable was the large amount of clothes, shoes and toys that appear for sale. There are two reasons for this. Firstly, there is a distinct lack of charity shops in France. So, the natural outlet for this type of unwanted gear is the Vide-Grenier.

Secondly, the price of clothes and shoes in the shops is outrageous; normally twice what you would expect in the UK. Therefore, the French folks wear their clothes and shoes till unusable and then pass them on at Vide-Greniers. I guess the popularity of toys goes the same way as the UK; bought at high cost, never used and finally sold on.

So, with our wide selection of stuff priced at low reasonable prices we could potentially make a killing. Our first attempt came at the large Vide-Grenier at Caylus. A yearly well attended event. It followed closely the completion of our first French language lessons, so it would be a good opportunity to try out our new skills. In fact I decided that, come what may, I would not reach for a dictionary nor make hand signals. It was all going to be in French!

Having set up our vast stall and priced everything up we waited for our first customer. He was not long in coming, here was my chance, my first attempt at fluent French, my chance to show off my grasp of the language.

"How can I help you?" I said in my slightly dodgy French.

At this point he reached into his pocket, brought out what looked like a microphone, put it to his throat and bleated out some unintelligible, Dalek sounding words, presumably in French.

Thus, for my first ever attempt at a 'French only' conversation I had picked the only guy in Caylus with no voice box! No doubt following a

Laryngectomy he had valiantly perfected the use of an electrolarynx to speak. And I am sure with other French folks this would have worked great. But to my ear it just sounded like interference on the radio.

So alas it was quickly back to hand signals and pointing to words in a dictionary. However, the rest of the day went very well, and we managed to sell a large quantity of unwanted stuff, most of which was finding its way on to the other French stalls at vastly increased prices. The French seem to have an interesting negotiation tactic, basically they don't.

First, they offer you a stupid low price for something already reasonably priced. This after perusing the object for ages, putting it down, picking it up and showing it to their partner. Your refusal of their stupid offer is met by much huffing, puffing, shocked looks and a shaking of the head. This is always followed by an overacted storming off.

A little later back they come again, this time they go through the same process of perusal but increase their offer a small amount. Your second refusal is greeted by a look of utter incredulity, had you really just refused his stupid offer again? And off they storm once more. Their third appearance normally results in the offer they should have started with, you accept, you shake hands and you are now great friends.

To combat folks who tried to wear us down throughout the day we adopted a 'three strikes and you're out' approach. If someone went beyond the three offers allowed, when they returned the fourth time, I simply said "It's sold." This nearly always resulted in a domestic in front of our stall as the wife berated her husband for being such a tight arse over something she wanted! I of course merely gave a Gallic shrug and turned to the next customer.

Our attempt at a Vide-Maison was also quite an experience. What we didn't anticipate was the number of villagers who came by just to be nosey. They seemed more interested in the contents of the house not for sale than the actual stuff we were trying to shift. However, a large amount of our unwanted accoutrements were slowly going.

After our Vide-Grenier experience we only allowed 2 strikes before switching someone off and this tactic seemed to be working well. Even electrical goods that had an English plug attached were being sold. They hadn't even noticed, and I was not going to point it out.

The high point of the day came when a farmer from a neighbouring village pointed to my extra-large metal ladders and asked, "How much?" Now these were big, heavy and I had never found a use for them so kept the price low. I just wanted to see them go. He knew a bargain when he saw one and immediately agreed my price, paid in cash and attempted to pick them up.

He struggled but waved off my offer of help. Now you have to picture the scene, these ladders were an extendable set of 3 and were about 4 metres high. A more hernia inducing combination you will never meet. He staggered from our farmhouse with the ladders towering above him; nearly collapsing several times on his way to his car.

It was at this stage that I realised that he just had a car; not a lorry or a van or even a trailer, just a car. And I thought that this weight might be a bit too much for just a roof rack. I needn't have worried; the car didn't have a roof rack!

As he approached his car, a rather nice-looking Peugeot hatchback, he let the ladders drop onto the roof, and balanced them nicely. After rummaging in the boot, he pulled out some rope and began to tie the ladders to the roof. This was done by passing the rope through the lowered windows. Was I really seeing this? Having secured the ladders to his now slightly dented car roof, he got inside and drove off!

As the car moved carefully away from our event the ladders rocked slowly up and down, each time denting the roof some more. You could actually hear the slightly crunching noise from 100 metres away. I have no idea of the result of his adventure as I never saw either himself or the car again. I wondered if perhaps his wife had murdered him when he got home!

About this time, I was hearing more and more about the forthcoming chasse season and all my new-found friends seemed to be heavily involved. Naturally they all wanted me to join, in fact Maurice, the Professor and Henri were all on the committee of the local chasse and were more than happy to help.

However, hunting is very much a divisive subject with many supporters and with many folks strongly against. For those who support it, the chasse is very important, almost a religion that is followed in any weather, any cost and whenever possible.

So, it is worth at this stage explaining something about the French chasse, both for and against and let you make up your own minds. I will not gloss over the details here so be prepared.

Firstly, let's be clear, we are not talking about a bunch of 'Hooray Henries' dressed in red jackets chasing about after foxes. I think it was Oscar

Wilde who said, "The unspeakable in full pursuit of the uneatable." I will leave that debate for the UK. Here in France the chasse is all about people from all backgrounds, especially from agriculture, hunting a limited number of animals who are in the food chain. They would all claim that this is not a sport but more of a necessity.

The animals in question being Sanglier *(wild boar)*, Chevreuil *(Roe deer)*, Cerf *(a large deer)*, Lapin *(rabbit)*, and Lièvre *(hare)*. However, foxes are regarded as vermin by the farmers thus during this chasse season they will be shot if seen. I will cover the birds such as Pheasant and Partridge towards the end.

The number of boar and deer shot is strictly controlled. This control being loosely based on the animal population which normally doubles each year. Thus, a target number of half the estimated population is the cut-off point. Once this number has been reached, at a given location, hunting there stops.

There are large numbers of boar and roe deer across France therefore the hunting activity normally lasts for the whole season; however, in some areas the large deer are in small numbers and are therefore hunted in very small numbers. As an example, with my local hunt we were only given permission to shoot one or two Cerf each season.

Each deer shot had to be tagged, numbered and recorded by sex, weight and health etc. This information continually being fed back to the chasse regional headquarters to enable a constant check on numbers. Each boar shot was recorded, and health checked to ensure that any illness was not getting into the food chain.

Every shot by a hunter whether a hit or a miss was recorded. This was very important as any miss could have wounded the animal and it was not permitted to simply leave a wounded animal to suffer. Therefore, at the end of the morning's hunt, teams of hunters with specially trained dogs would follow any trail where an animal may have been wounded. This normally led to any wounded animal being quickly found and dispatched.

The most common method of hunting animals is the Battue *(a hunting method that provides a clear shot at the prey)* Hunters are stationed at various agreed points and stand waiting as beaters with specially trained packs of dogs *(the Meute)* basically chase about making a lot of noise. The dogs have an incredible sense of smell and once a scent has been picked up they will chase off barking. This will result in the boar or deer to run in the opposite direction towards the waiting hunters.

At the end of a Battue, normally a Sunday morning, the dead boar or deer will be collected and butchered ready for joint distribution that afternoon. After a somewhat lengthy lunch *(more about that later)* the hunters will return, and the joints of meat shared out amongst all those who had attended. As you would expect, the best cuts going to any hunter who had actually shot something that morning.

As for the bird shoots well, these are somewhat different. Pheasant and partridge are no longer found in large numbers across rural France, thus are bought in large numbers and let loose before a hunt day. This is called the lâcher *(basically the let go)*.

Different species are allowed to be hunted on different days and again strict control is kept on numbers. Migratory birds such as the 'bécasse' *(woodcock)* are very carefully regulated due to reducing numbers.

It's perhaps worth mentioning some of the hunting pros and cons as seen by the French. We will start with some pros.

Hunting in France is very much a tradition but also has an indispensable element. I have already mentioned that the population of both boar and deer double each year. What would happen without the hunt? Last year saw 23,000 road accidents involving wild animals, 70% involving deer and some 24% with wild boar. With no hunt a yearly cull would be required leading to exactly the same hunt scenario.

Forgetting the road accidents, you must also bear in mind the incredible damage that wild boar do to crops. A large family of wild boar can destroy several fields of crops in just one night as they dig for grubs and roots etc. And of course, foxes are regarded as the perennial pest that create havoc to most farming activities as well as spreading disease.

Having an official hunting season controls who has got a firearm, how they get them, where they keep them and more importantly how they use them. There is a tough examination process before you can become a hunt member. This includes both theoretical and practical elements.

There are very strict rules on where you can discharge your weapon, how you discharge your weapon and why. All hunting activity must be clearly marked on any route warning both drivers and walkers that a hunt is in progress. All hunters must wear high visibility clothing to make their activity very clear. I guess lastly and least important, the hunters really enjoy hunting.

So, on to some of the more obvious cons as seen by anti-hunt folks. Hunting is extremely dangerous. Every year sees both hunters and non-hunters killed or injured due to a hunting accident. For example, at the start of this year's hunting season, a Brit was shot dead as he cycled through a forest where a hunt was in progress.

The hunters walk all over the place, in and out of people's private land, their dogs running wild with no respect to personal property. The hunters are often drunk and shouldn't be in charge of any sort of weapon. There is no control over what they shoot at or where they shoot. The killing of innocent animals is totally barbaric and unnecessary in today's modern age.

You can see the dilemma, those 'for' have lots of positives and those 'against' can find lots of negatives. All I can say is let's have a look at driving a car. A very strict test with lots of controlled important rules to follow yet we still have accidents. People are breathalysed and found drunk, people speed and take chances. In other words, in every activity there will be idiots and idiots cause accidents.

The only point 'against' that I personally find difficult to understand is the point about killing animals. If this argument is coming from a vegetarian or a vegan then hands up, you may have a point. But when it comes from a meat eater, someone who is happy for someone else to slaughter their meat, wrap it up nicely or disguise it as something else, then no.

My view on all this was steered by my desire for integration and to experience the true French life. And if that meant joining the chasse, so be it. I certainly was not going to jump on one side of the fence, or the other, without looking from the inside. As proof that this strategy works, after many years of living in France, I am now more sympathetic towards the anti-hunt stance than when I started.

So, after the period of my chasse apprenticeship, as mentioned in the first chapter, my next hurdle was the entry examinations. These take place a few times a year and I had to sign on with the Chasse Federation to book my place. And of course, pay a fee and buy a book. For a moment I thought I would be leaving with two carrier bags! What I did not anticipate was the complexity of what was required.

You are given a large book packed with security rules, wildlife species, their habitats, their food chain, their numbers of offspring, their migration patterns. It then went on to hunting styles and practices, dog breeds, their specialisms and care. Then on to weapons, the different types, the ammunition, cleaning, security and so on and so on.

I have one of my old Chasse books in front of me, it runs to 383 pages! Did I really need to know how long a Perdrix Bartavelle sits on its eggs for? Apparently, yes.

You can see my problem, apparently lots of French folks fail this examination and they happen to speak French. I, on the other hand, quite obviously didn't. I explained this slight setback to the Mayor who told me to check out the Chasse Federation website. Apparently, you could try the theory examination on line to test your knowledge.

"So, I can try this exam on line and see the questions?" I asked.

"Not all the questions," he replied, "you will get 21 questions and you need to get at least 16 correct to pass."

"So, they only show 21 of their questions thus you can only try this once?" I rather disappointedly replied.

"No," came his puzzled answer, "each time you attempt it you will get a different set of questions."

"How many questions have they got in total?" I enquired, now realising that I was actually talking to the only man in France that would know the answer.

"390," he said, "all in different categories."

"But be careful," he continued, "there are some questions that, if you get wrong, are an immediate failure of the whole exam."

This was now becoming very French; a possible 21 questions out of a total of 390, but you could access them all by continually trying the examination on line. So, I forgot the book and hit the internet. By about the 30th time I tried the test, I passed, but I kept going. Very quickly it became clear where the 'immediate failure' questions were; and as you would expect they were all security or safety based.

The more I tried the test the better score I achieved and very soon it 21/21 every time. Now you could call this cheating but actually, by osmosis, I had learned most of the information in the book by heart. A bit like an actor learns his lines except I was getting tested on mine.

The day of the examination arrived, and I turned up at the Federation in good time. On arrival though it was obvious that I would not be alone, about 30 or so likeminded individuals were milling about at the locked door.

Here's another peculiarity with French folks, they can't queue. If there is not a queue forming, they will mill about and when a door opens will rush to the front. With, I might add, much pushing and shoving. If there is a queue forming somewhere, they will simply walk to the front and look most surprised and hurt if you push them away. What is even more interesting is that this is not just youngsters lacking respect, it is normally the more mature folks who should know better.

Back at the Federation, at the appointed time the door opened and on cue *(see what I did there)* they all rushed in. I followed up and took my seat as the multi-choice answer papers were being handed out. Multi-choice? This was getting easier by the minute. There was a deathly quiet in the room, none of the usual banter that you get when a group of guys get together; they were all a bit tense. Then the test began.

The questions commenced by being projected onto a large screen, and thankfully they were identical to the ones shown on the Federation website. Being multi-choice made no difference to me as I knew all the answers anyway, but they should have made it easier for some; it didn't.

At the end of the examination all the answer papers were handed in and we had to wait while they were checked. But this is France, no note in the post with your results, no email to say if you were successful or had failed, you were going to be told right now.....in front of everyone else!

One by one a name was called out with the resulting score. Unbelievably some of the candidates were failing but most had passed. Two of us had achieved 100% and received a round of applause, plus our first year's Federation fee for free.

A rather puzzled look came on the face of one of the failed candidates when he discovered that I could hardly string a complete sentence together in French. I now had discovered two things; firstly the French are not great internet users. Secondly, I now knew how the mayor had achieved his 21/21 and he never boasted of it again.

The practical examination went much the same way with practice sessions at the Federation's shooting site leading to a test. I have to admit I learned a great deal about the security and general firing of weapons at these sessions.

However, I remained a rubbish shot, a personal feature that I was relying on so as not to actually shoot anything!

CHAPTER EIGHT

Barney the Dog and On the Chasse

"You will need a dog," said the Professor.

"I've already got two dogs," I explained, while casually pointing to our two Miniature Schnauzers snoozing in the shade.

"No, a real dog," he continued, with much waving of hands that somehow represented a real dog.

"They are real dogs," I said, "they bark and everything."

"But they don't hunt, you need a hunting dog," he continued, this time giving the visual representation of a dog hunting!

Maurice could only agree with this logic and, as he re-measured the distance between my pétanque boule and the piglet, he proposed the solution. Apparently one of the elderly hunters from Caylus had an English Setter that had just given birth to a litter of pups.

"I'm not sure," I said, "anyway, they are going to be expensive."

"Not at all," he replied, "he will give them away to other hunters."

Now in the UK an English Setter pup could set you back £1,000 so this 'give away' scenario didn't make sense. Also, I still wasn't sure that this would be wise, even if I could persuade my wife that this was a good idea.

"Are you telling me that he will give them away for nothing?" I questioned.

"No, of course not," he explained, "you will need to give him bag of Croques."

(Croques or Croquettes is the word that the French use for, what we would call, dry dog food. It comes in many qualities from very cheap, probably saw dust; up to expensive, probably very nutritious.)

"Anyway," I said, "my wife would not be happy with another dog."

"Just tell her he will bucket them if he can't find homes," he replied, thus completing his logical French answer to my problem.

Two months later we were the proud owners of an English Setter puppy called Barney and our lives would never be the same again, he was completely barking mad. "Don't worry," I would say, "he will calm down when he gets a bit older." Eleven years later this excuse is wearing a bit thin and the only saving grace is that he now sleeps most of the time and has gracefully retired from hunting.

Our 'cheap' dog promise also proved to be a bit of a fallacy. Barney did indeed cost me a bag of Croques *(very large, best quality)* and I also added a very large bottle of Ricard. Unfortunately, at the age of 5 it appeared that Barney was a diabetic, no real reason, just one of those things. However, the cost of insulin and other medication is high thus, so far, my freebie French dog has cost me about £8,000!

The immediate reaction to this bottle of Ricard was the owner opening the bottle and insisting we all get stuck in. And as usual it was hard to get away as he could not understand my reluctance to drink more than one Ricard. This was despite my overacted 'driving a car' mime.

However, he did have some interesting hunting 'souvenirs' hanging around the room, including a World War Two machine gun. I assume that was used for hunting Germans!

We also had quite a debate about our chosen doggy name, well this is France and even naming something is complex.

"What are you going to call him?" asked the owner.

"Barney," we said, carefully avoiding the bit about Barney Rubble being rhyming slang for 'trouble'. Very prophetic as it happens but too difficult to explain with our struggling French.

"You can't," he said, "it has to be a D."

"Er, so why does it have to be a D?" we asked, now completely baffled.

"Because it's a D year," he continued, as if this explained everything.

I closed this debate by saying "Oui" with the usual thumbs up; we refused yet another Ricard and drove off with 'B' for Barney.

On further investigation we found out that for about 100 years the French registry for dogs has followed an alphabet system for naming dogs that are actually registered with themselves. This apparently makes it easy to age a dog by its name.

Eliminating K, Q, W, X, Y and Z due to lack of name choice, left a 20-year repeating choice of letters. D, of course, corresponded to that year which was 2008. However, we were not going to register any names, but by naming him Barney we had just added a couple of years to his age. Luckily, he will never know!

Henri was impressed with Barney but confused when I asked him how best to train him. His view was that he will not need training, he will know what to do instinctively. That is unless he is scared by guns. If that was the case, apparently, he would never hunt.

This was a bit of a shock, had I just taken on a hunting dog that actually had the potential of never hunting? I had to put this to the test, I also had to dream up an excuse for the wife in case of this 'worse case' scenario. It had to be better than the 'bucket' solution as, after the first three weeks with Barney, she was close to doing that herself anyway!

So out in the fields I went, threw him a ball, shot my gun in the air and he completely ignored the gunshot and retrieved the ball. He had passed the test. And in fact, went on to be quite an incredible hunter. To show how lucky this was, his father turned out to be frightened of shotgun noises and never actually hunted. He ended up as a house pet for the owner's son continually causing chaos in Loser!

Barney would often show up other hunting dogs who had wandered past us with their owners. It was not unusual for these hunters to have 3 or 4 dogs each and they zigzagged across the fields searching for pheasant. Barney would sit patiently for them to pass, zip into the field where they had just searched and flush up a bird. His sense of smell seemed to reach 50 metres or more and he never failed.

In fact, the only failure was my aim, if I missed a bird that he had found he would slowly look round with a 'you twat' look. Then he would be off again in search of the next bird. It was quite apparent that the only training needed here was me. He still gives me that same 'you twat' look, only now it's when I wake him up to go for a walk!

Barney's greatest achievement was when he upstaged me in a hugely popular French hunting magazine, 'Plaisirs de la Chasse.' *(Basically the pleasures of hunting.)* I had been contacted by a journalist who had somehow found out that I was a member of the chasse, something of a rarity for a Brit at the time.

She was doing an article on foreigners who join the hunt and wanted to come and interview me. A date was agreed, and she turned up and immediately fell in love with Barney. All her questions seemed to be Barney based and I was beginning to wonder if this was a stitch up.

Finally, after much discussion we got around to photographs for the magazine. And, of course, Barney took centre stage with me as something of an add-on.

After she had all she needed we shook hands, and as a parting shot she gave the date of the actual publication of the story. However, she appeared to be looking at Barney as she said it, and to this day I am sure that he nodded in response.

The date of the magazine's monthly publication soon arrived, and I rushed out to get my copy. There was indeed an article and a photograph, mostly about Barney. She even called him Monsieur Barney. And just to rub salt into the wounds she had spelt my name wrong! My plan to buy a copy for all of my friends suddenly went out of the window!

With my chasse membership secured I was invited as a guest to the Camp Caylus Battue. This was a big hunt involving some 200 hunters covering the vast private terrain that made up the military training camp at Caylus. Being a 'military only' area this was a hunter's paradise as it was completely unpopulated, untouched for hundreds of years and overfull of wildlife.

The reason the military allowed the hunt on their terrain was to reduce the number of accidents. These were constant due to wild sanglier and deer running in front of army vehicles causing crashes.

The camp had some interesting history some say dating back to the Roman battles against the Gauls. It later formed a medieval fortress and eventually a military camp.

It was used by the French Vichy government to intern foreign workers during the war. After the war it was used as a holding camp for German POWs and then a prison for Vietnamese captives during the French Vietnam war. A somewhat chequered history.

It was finally named Camp Lieutenant Colonel Normand after the last senior officer during the war years. He orchestrated the hiding of 30 tonnes of arms and munitions from the Germans but was betrayed by someone. He was arrested and sent to Buchenwald concentration camp where he later died.

So how does one of these hunts actually work and can the French, with their hundreds of years of hunting experience, successfully run one? The answer is…sort of.

The day starts early with a large gathering of folks at the hunting lodge, and as you would expect with a large gathering of French hunting folk, it looked like an army battalion. I don't know who is selling this ex-army gear, but they are making a fortune.

My hand was beginning to ache as I followed my host, Maurice, around shaking hands and saying bonjour to everyone there. He took great delight in announcing to all that I was English; apparently, I was the first English guy to join the hunt in the region.

This, of course, made me stand out and become somewhat of a mascot over time. It also led to one guy after another coming over and show off a few words of their very bad English. Luckily the 'I am playing tennis' guy was not there!

At this stage I felt a bit sorry for anyone arriving from Scotland, Northern Ireland or Wales. It was clear that any person who speaks English and comes from the UK was English. Not only that, but they must have lived in London, mustn't they? If I had said that actually I am

Scottish, they would still have thought that I lived in London!

Much is made of checking the hunting permits, paying fees, checking what location you had been allocated and arguing. People scrambled to check the results pinned up from the previous hunt while others poured out a very stewed black coffee.

Yes, correct, the Professor was in charge of the giant coffee urn; the very same machine that he misused at the Loto evening.

Most of this was happening inside the lodge which once was an old farmhouse and now served as the base for hunting at Camp Caylus. There was no way this was big enough for everyone, but they continued to crowd in, all choking on the smoky atmosphere.

At one end a very large open fireplace burned with a pile of damp logs causing much heat, but equally causing much smoke to generate around the room. In fact, from several paces it was very hard to actually read the 'No Smoking' sign casually hung on the wall!

Meanwhile the chasse 'Garde Particulier' *(hunt guard)* wandered about trying to look very important in his military style uniform. His name was Jano, or at least that is what everyone called him. He was in his early seventies, small in stature but big in heart. The sort of guy that always had a smile even when things were going wrong.....which was often.

His uniform had seen better days and looked quite battered, a peaked military hat slightly bent, a Garde Particulier jumper with a battered badge and finally a jacket that was obviously issued to him before he had put on a few pounds!

(The hunt guard is in charge of checking paperwork and ensuring that everyone sticks to the very rigid rules during a hunt. This could be a Battue or a bird shoot.)

In typical French fashion no account seemed to have been made of how best to accomplish all this initial checking. In fact the hunters had to queue several times to achieve what could easily have been completed by queuing just once. And all this time they were choking on the fire fumes; however, at least they were queuing.

I suddenly realised that, by luck, some of my new-found friends had a big part to play here, and were very much in control. All except the Mayor, he just strolled up and down looking as though he would like to line them all up for inspection. I noticed that he was treated with some reverence with nods and a 'mon colonel' instead of bonjour.

It transpired that his last job before retirement was Commandant of Camp Caylus. Thus, I was in a good position here, one that would lead eventually to me being voted onto the Chasse Committee.

Last to arrive at the lodge were the 'Meute' *(dog pack)* owners. The dogs themselves were in two different categories, those who chase and those who track potentially wounded animals. Most were caged into converted trailers and were making quite a racket. They obviously were very keen to get going.

It was hard for me, as a dog owner myself, to see the condition of some of these dogs. Some were very well cared for, but a few clearly were not. This was something that I did try to address later during my time on the committee.

The dog pack owners and their 'beater' helpers do a very dangerous job. They are often in the line of fire between the hunters and potential targets. Due to this they wear a large amount of fluorescent clothing, but they are in danger from two directions. First from shots from the hunters, second from disturbing an angry sanglier at close quarters. However, I admit that it is the hunt dogs who are continually in the most danger.

The danger of accidents is somewhat mitigated by the use of 'miradors.' *(a small wooden tower)* These raise the hunters about 1.5 metres off the ground thus, in theory, the shot is always pointed downwards. The hunters always bring along a plank of wood to place on the mirador to act as a bench seat for the hunt.

If you ever wondered what these towers were, as you drove through rural France, now you know.

I tried this meute activity once when Jacques, one of the better known local meute owners, invited me to join his group for a Sunday hunt. I was petrified for most of the morning and felt as though I had a big target stuck on my back. Also, his tales of being gored by sangliers didn't help, he made it sound as though this was a certainty rather than a rare occurrence.

Back at the lodge; by now with all the hunters, organisers, meute owners, trackers, beaters and me, it was getting a bit crowded. Suddenly there was a loud hunting horn blast, and all were called to order.

Henri was stood with a prepared list of 'must do's' and after much fussing by another committee member he was wired for sound. The microphone didn't work of course and was rearranged several times in between much booing and 'zuts', plus a few 'putains'.

In all the years that I attended this hunt scenario they never actually managed to get the microphone to work properly. This always just generated much laughter and you could see the Mayor cringe as he felt that someone should be put on jankers. So, with much shouting Henri went through his list.

What could be shot and what could not.

The need to clearly identify the animal before shooting.

What time it started and what time it finished.

How to signal if a Cerf had been shot.

(Only one allocated to be shot for this whole season, thus once this had been achieved only the hunting of chevreuil would be allowed. In fact, over the many years that I participated in the Caylus hunt only one Cerf was actually shot.)

How to indicate that a shot had missed.

What to do when a car or van passed by the hunters.

What type of gun was allowable.

What type of ammunition was allowable.

Absolutely no alcohol before or during the hunt.

How the meat would be shared and when.

And so on and so on, these folks had listened to this for years, but the rules were clear, before each hunt they had to read through the rules.

Then another blast on the horn and off they all went, the meute owners to their start points and the hunters to their allocated miradors. White vans and four-by-fours were disappearing faster than snow on a hot summer's day. And very soon there was just me standing there.

This left about 45 minutes before the start of the hunt and I was looking for the Professor as he would be taking me to my spot, next to his. He was nowhere to be found, nor was Maurice, nor was the Mayor, even Henri seemed to have disappeared. Suddenly Jano poked his head through the lodge door and through the escaping smoke he signalled for me to come in.

Suddenly the tables that had served as document checking positions had been converted into a buffet breakfast. And the hunt organisers, committee and a few privileged folks were tucking in.

A large number of baguettes, big lumps of cheese, jars of homemade pâté, some well-watered-down wine, *(it would appear that if they couldn't have alcohol, they just went for something that looked like it!)* slabs of ham, sausages, and finally some drinkable coffee. So, the French aren't that daft, they didn't let the Professor anywhere near their private coffee machine.

This was a veritable feast and their pocket knives were slashing backwards and forwards as they sliced off chunks of meat and cheese to pop in the torn-up baguettes. On a more serious note walkie-talkies were being handed out to keep track of the day's proceedings. Okay....this is France, they call them talkie-walkies!

(It's worth just breaking off here for a moment to mention something about pocket knives in France. The French have an absolute fascination with knives, well at least the guys do. Most carry them, normally very sharp and nearly always of the regional variety.

In fact, when the tables were laid for the hunt lunch, later in the day, the first thing I noticed was that there were forks but no knives laid out. It was just assumed that everyone would have their own 'preferred' knife.

Probably the most famous of these knives in France is the Opinel, a basic wooden handled folding knife originating from the Savoie region. You see them for sale everywhere and they are cheap compared to some of their competitors.

Perhaps the most famous worldwide is the traditional Laguiole pocket knife. Like the Opinel it dates back to the 19th century, this time coming from the Aveyron. They can be priced quite cheaply but quickly rise in price to the hundreds of euros. Always with an easily identifiable shape and distinctive bee shape on the back, they are a French icon. Most regions in France boast of a regional pocket knife shape.

As with the UK there are strict laws regarding the carrying of knives but if the blade does not have a locking mechanism and it is of reasonable size, they are legal. But why carry a knife? You may ask. Well to begin with in France it is very much part of their culture. They have always carried them.

Next, they are incredibly handy. I use mine all the time to cut through the incessant packaging that covers everything you buy, make quick *repairs to stuff that goes wrong and prune plants in the garden. Also, and this is a major reason, beef in France is totally inedible unless you have a very sharp knife to attack it with.*

So, if you go to a restaurant and order a steak, get ready for a struggle unless you can cut it up into thin slices. - I am reliably informed that this is because French butchers do not hang their meat!

As a result of all this, it is quite usual to see French guys comparing their knives and discussing in some detail the pros and cons of each type.

They were absolutely intrigued by my rather nice Soligen knife, noting its amazing quality manufacture, high quality blade and nicely finished stag horn handle. That was right up to the moment I mentioned that Soligen is actually in Germany.....then it was crap!)

With the impromptu breakfast over, and with the actual start of the hunt getting dangerously close, we packed up, jumped in our cars and headed off. The camp terrain is massive and without a good knowledge of the layout you could easily get lost.

Therefore, I was lucky to have a guide. We drove past rows of miradors where hunters tried valiantly to make themselves comfortable for the 4-hour long hunt duration.

It was cold and a bit wet so large umbrellas were going up, huge coats were being put on, and guns were being checked and quickly placed down as we passed. Already we could hear the distant howling of the dogs as they strained at the leash to set off.

As we drove past the mirador with Jean-Pierre in attendance, I noticed that he was simply stood there with his normal summer jacket on. The only difference to the norm being a rather shabby fluorescent cap.

We parked up and made it to our miradors just in time as hunting horns could be heard relaying the start of the hunt. Too close for comfort for me but the Professor didn't seem troubled at all. I climbed up onto my mirador, put up my umbrella, put down my seat, loaded my shotgun with a slug, and waited and waited.

(Shotguns normally shoot a large number of small round balls or 'shot' that spread out quickly over distance. This literally is to maximise the ability to hit a bird travelling fast through the air.

However for big game, either a sanglier or chevreuil, a large lead bullet or slug is used.

This has the impact ability of a clean kill, albeit less than accurate beyond 50 metres. Most of the hunters prefer a rifle which has greater accuracy over distance.)

You have a very strict shooting zone which I will try to describe. Imagine a narrow road with woods on both sides. Along one side of the road every 50 metres or so stands a mirador. So, stood on your mirador if you looked left then right you would see a line of other miradors disappearing along the road.

You judge 30 degrees up from your right-hand neighbour to the land in front of you; then the same again up from your left-hand neighbour. The land in between this measurement is your personal shooting zone, and any legal animal appearing in that area is yours to shoot; after of course clear identification.

To correctly make this measurement you can pace out the required distances for 30 degrees and mark off the ground to indicate your reference area. Luckily this had nearly always been done by a previous hunter thus from your mirador position you could clearly see the limit of your own zone. If all this does not make sense…you can only shoot ahead not to the side for obvious reasons!

Hunting like fishing can be a very boring business, with many hours sat watching with not a lot happening. This boredom is interspersed with short periods of excitement as action suddenly explodes out of nowhere. I had sat for about 2 hours and was beginning to daydream when suddenly I heard, what can only be described as, a tank coming through the undergrowth behind me.

I did not know what it was, but it was making a terrific racket and approaching fast. There were no dogs howling and no beaters shouting just a lot of loud crunching noises and it was getting nearer.

Suddenly out of the undergrowth, right next to the Professor, a large herd of sanglier rushed out at speed and headed for the woods on the other side of the road. *(a sounder of boars? a herd of boar?...whatever!)* Far too quick for me to react but they were right next to the Professor, yet he didn't budge. I waved and shouted so did the hunter to his other side; with no effect.

So, to recap about 20 large lumbering sanglier had just run past the Professor and disappeared into the woods on the other side of the road. It quickly became obvious that he was asleep, fast asleep, nothing was going to wake him up. In fact, he only woke again when the horns finally sounded for the end of the hunt.

"Why didn't you shoot?" I asked.

"Shoot what?" he responded looking a bit puzzled.

"One of the 20 or so sanglier who ran right past you," I replied.

"What sanglier?" he continued, now looking a bit indignant.

"I bet you was asleep," I said, simply as the obvious answer.

"Rubbish, I never sleep when I'm hunting," he replied, and with that he packed up his gear and wandered back to the car.

"Why didn't he shoot?" said the Professor's other hunting neighbour.

"Best not mention it," I said!

During the hunt there was obviously much activity with the organisers. A van had driven by twice to enquire if anything had been shot at and missed. These were the teams with the trained 'search and find' dogs that would be used to locate any wounded animal.

If someone had missed a shot, marks would be clearly made in the ground to indicate the direction the animal took. Then immediately the hunt was over these dogs would return and ensure that no animal had been left wounded in the undergrowth.

Also, a van pulling a trailer had continually circulated the hunting terrain retrieving any sanglier or chevreuil that had been killed. These were taken back to the lodge for checking before being butchered for joints of meat.

The rules when these vehicles pass are quite clear. As one passes, the hunter on the mirador makes their weapon safe until the vehicle has passed by. On one famous occasion, a few years after I had started the hunt, Caylus had been visited by some of the senior hunt Federation Marshals.

They were on their usual round of checking each and every hunt in the Tarn et Garonne. The purpose being to ensure that everyone was following the rules and regulations. Due to increasing anti-hunt political lobbies they just could not afford to allow any problems.

Unfortunately, as a white van trundled slowly in front of Jean-Pierre, a sanglier appeared on the other side of the road. With the van immediately in front of him, Jean-Pierre raised his shotgun and fired at the sanglier. The bullet whizzed past the van missing it by inches, also missing the sanglier.

The van braked hard, stopped and out stepped the now ashen faced Federation Marshal. He walked up to Jean-Pierre, confiscated his shotgun and told him to sit where he was until the end of the hunt. He would not be getting his gun back until this hunt was over. The subsequent hearing about the incident saw Jean-Pierre lose his hunting licence for the rest of the season.

The only reason he did not lose it completely was due to his need as a farmer to have a shotgun on his land, he was very lucky. However, he was so scared of his mother that he did not tell her that he had lost his licence. So, whenever there was a bird hunt, he could be seen with his dogs leaving his house, shotgun over his shoulder but no ammunition.

Whenever there was a Battue, he would leave his house and disappear for the day. I can only assume that he took meat out of his freezer and presented it again as the spoils of his day's labours. When I questioned him about this he just laughed and made a cutting motion across his throat. I assume that would have been his punishment if his mother had found out!

As for us back at that first hunt, well we were on our way back to the lodge for the traditional end of hunt meal. Most of the hunters at this stage made their way to one of the many sheds, shacks or lean-to's that were scattered all over the camp. And there they would make a bar-b-que for a lengthy lunch while waiting for the allotted meat sharing time.

This was a time to share stories of how they missed the biggest sanglier you have ever seen, how they had shot at point blank range and missed something due to the poor manufacture of ammunition these days, how they had seen nothing all day due to the incompetence of the meute teams, how the committee had given them rubbish mirador locations out of spite, and generally how they would never come back again unless things improved. So, business as usual then.

As we pulled up at the lodge, I realised yet again the privileged position I was in. Only a few non-committee members were actually eating in the lodge, like the Mayor, a few Federation officials and....well me. Someone had returned early and set everything up and already apero's were disappearing fast. It was either Ricard or Scotch Whisky, they have a real love of Scotch Whisky and drink an awful lot of the stuff.

They also have a great love of their 'Eau-de-Vie,' *(water of life)* the normally homemade strong alcoholic drink. I did try to educate them on the name coincidence but failed somewhere in the translation.

(Basically, the word whisky derives from the Gaelic word 'uisce' in Ireland or 'uisge' in Scotland, both meaning water. The Latin for alcohol 'aqua vitae' translates to water of life and soon we saw 'uisge beatha' meaning water of life in Scotland. This pronunciation of 'uisge' simply became whisky… there you go, water of life all round then!

Whilst the homemade production of strong spirits is illegal in most of the world, this is France; therefore they have to be different. Due to a law dating back to the 1920s, fruit growers and their offspring were given the right to produce 20 litres at 50% proof of the fruit based Eau-de-Vie. This was tax free but for their own consumption.

The right to do this was withdrawn eventually but while those offspring still live, they retain the right. And Jano was one of the offspring!)

So back at the lodge, with much boasting about how wonderful they were at hunting, miming of shooting at something and comparing their knives, the attendees sat down at the table for the hunt lunch.

The committee took it in turns to provide the lunch and today it was the turn of the Professor. At a later date I took my turn and they all asked for something traditionally English. So, I made a large pan of Chicken Masala curry.

It was a first for all of them, but they seemed to enjoy it, even though the French do not do spice. Actually seeing them wrestle with poppadoms was hilarious. At the next event one of the hunt committee told me that he had spent that whole week with a 'bouchon' *(cork)* stuck up his arse!

While they all compared knives yet again, and explained why my German one was a disaster, the Professor handed out what looked like a huge blob of jelly with a hard-boiled egg floating in the middle. It turned out to be a huge blob of jelly with a hard-boiled egg floating in the middle!

This was our starter and given my dislike of all things jelly it could not have started off much worse. I do not know what the culinary term is for this dish and I do not want to know, it was not looking good.

Meanwhile baguettes were being torn to bits with much debris going everywhere and the wine was flowing. Thankfully the wine was not Jean-Pierre's and was actually drinkable. One of the guests was a local dentist who had a never-ending stream of dirty jokes. I always understood the first line, then he would speed up as it got to the punchline. Everyone would roar with laughter and I would be left looking blank.

If he saw me look blank, he would say the punchline again at twice the decibels, this time I would fake comprehension and laugh. This was simply to avoid getting to such a decibel rating that someone would end up deaf!

The main course was chicken, well several chickens actually and the chosen vegetable was chips. Now I don't mean chips as we know them. Chips happens to be the French term for crisps. Yes, our chosen vegetable was several large bags of crisps.

All the time this bizarre meal was going on the Hunt Guard, Jano, was receiving calls from the 'search and find' teams to announce that a shot animal had been located. His job then was to ensure that the retrieval van left to collect the animal for the butchering process.

Unfortunately, Jano was a bit deaf and these calls were taken with much shouting from himself as he tried to hear the call over the noise from our fellow diners. Also, unfortunately for Jano, each time he got back to the table and lifted a fork to his mouth, one member of the committee inside the lodge would call Jano's mobile phone number. As he lowered his fork again to take the call, they would say that they were out being chased by a sanglier.

There followed a shouted debate about what they should do while everyone else in the room fell about laughing. Finally, he would look up and shout 'salaud' *(bastard)* and get on with his meal.

He fell for this joke countless times for years, unfortunately sometimes shouting 'salaud' when someone was actually having a real problem.

I followed my Jean-Pierre's meal modus operandi by taking the breast of chicken as my choice, again this was greeted by 'what a polite chap' nods. Meanwhile out of the corner of my eye I could see the Professor greedily munching on a chicken head.

There followed the traditional cheese and bread which I managed to turn into an argument when I mentioned that they were eating it at the wrong time.

"Cheese should really be eaten at the end of a meal," I casually mentioned.

"What? That's disgusting," came the universal reply.

I did make sure that the French ate their cheese at the end of any meal they had at our house. And after a few occasions, with an accompanying Brandy or Port, they seemed to get very used to it!

With a piece of supermarket gateaux making up the dessert, the hunt meal was over, and it was time for coffee and an Eau-de-Vie. As it was someone's birthday a bottle or two of Champagne had also been produced.

"Ah, English fizz," I said, knowing that this would result in uproar.

"What do you mean English Fizz?" came the obvious response.

"Sparkling wine was invented in England by an Englishman," I answered, a fact actually told to me by a French vineyard owner.

They decided that I must be joking and started to share out the Champers. I didn't have the heart to mention that the wine they had all been drinking was actually American!

(A recipe for the deliberate production of sparkling wine was recorded in 1698 by a

Gloucester doctor, Christopher Merret. This was some 20 years before the French Benedictine monk and cellar master, Dom Pierre Perignon, had recorded his.

As to the wine, well following the great French wine blight in the mid-19th century, the French wine industry was all but destroyed. It was caused by an Aphid that had originated in North America and brought across the Atlantic by the various trading ships.

No amount of pesticide would solve the problem and the only solution was to graft aphid-resistant American vines across all the damaged French vineyards. So, the next time someone mentions how wonderful their French wine is, you can remind them that that are actually drinking American wine!)

Back with the Eau-de-Vie, this was Jano's moment, out he came with a large bottle that was wearing a knitted jacket. On the stopper at the top of the bottle was a woolly hat and he placed it with pride in the centre of the table. Everyone was taking some, either into their coffee or neat, thus I had no choice I poured some into a glass.

Have you ever had to syphon petrol out of your car only to swallow a bit as you sucked on the syphon tube? Yes? Okay, you now know what it tasted like. Everyone else seemed to enjoy it though.

A few years later I took my friend Eric on the hunt and had to walk him outside as he lifted a large glass of this stuff towards his lips. Quickly making him pour it on the grass we went back inside to join the fun. So, mate, I saved your life!

On one occasion while Jano was outside organising retrieval vans, the guys on the inside emptied his woolly coated bottle into an empty plastic bottle. They then filled his Eau-de-Vie bottle with water and carried on as usual. Jano went home that day thinking that he had a nearly full bottle of Eau-de-Vie left.

He apparently, with much ceremony, put his woolly coated bottle on the table at home following a big family meal occasion. Faces were pulled, strange looks were passed all round and accusing looks given to Jano. I am told that you could hear the shout of 'les salauds' from at least a kilometre away!

It was now just a matter of waiting for the butchers to finish their work before all the hunt attendees returned for their share of the meat. I took this opportunity to watch them at work, not for the faint hearted I might add but I wanted the full-on experience.

They were very professional and fast. It really did not take very long for an animal to be converted into joints of meat and not much was wasted. I noted that even the sanglier heads were being kept as these would be cooked for the cheeks and brains.

(It rather reminded me of when I went on my first business trip to France with my friend Pete. We were in a Paris restaurant confronted by a menu all in French with zero understanding of what it all meant.

I went for the Steak Tartare because...well they can't screw up a steak can they? Pete went for Cervelle de Veau because he had a little book that informed him that Veau was French for calf...what could possibly go wrong?

To give him his due, the waiter pointed to his own head several times after Pete had ordered his Veau. The less Pete responded the more animated the waiter became, finally giving a shrug and walking off.

Of course, I ended up with a plate of raw mince with a nice raw egg balanced on top and Pete got his plate of brains!)

We finally got to the allotted time for meat distribution. It was nearly 17.00 and I had been up since 06.00, it had already been a long day and it was about to become longer.

So, how do you share out 200 joints of meat amongst 200 or so tired, cold, irritated and wet Frenchmen? In the most ridiculously long and tedious fashion of course!

To make the distribution fair the joints of meat had been placed in a vast group of numbered pigeon holes. Each joint placed inside a white carrier bag. While this was being done by the butchers, the committee, inside the hunting lodge, were allocating a number to each hunter by pulling names out of a hat.

The plan was to allocate one piece of meat anonymously to each hunter, and two for any hunter who had actually shot an animal. Yes, you've got it, a successful hunter would be walking off with two carrier bags!

Chalk boards had been written up to indicate what animal had been shot, where and by who. This just seemed to upset everyone as they felt that the best places had been given to the chosen few. The fact that no one had told the animals where those chosen few were standing seemed to have escaped their attention!

The next problem was that they had started this allocation process late in the afternoon, thus everyone was hanging around for ages for it to finish. Then they started to call out each name in Alphabetical order. As your name was called out you walked up to the distribution area and collected your carrier bag containing your meat. You then wandered off.

As I saw this commence, I realised that those at the end of the alphabet were in for a very long wait. In fact, everyone was in for a very long wait due to the sound system that continued to fail amongst much shouting, 'zutting' and general mayhem.

There were also a large number of hunters who were clearly not satisfied with their meat allocation. "Why did I get ribs again when that guy over there has got a leg of sanglier?" "This isn't the leg from the chevreuil I shot, it's too small!" and so on. Nobody seemed happy and everyone had a better way of doing it!

At least they altered the direction of the alphabet from week to week else, if your name began with a 'Z', you could be stuck there for days.

Finally, we got to the end of the whole laborious process and it was time to hose everything down, clean up and go home. About 50 animals had been killed with a 50/50 ratio of sanglier to chevreuil. I thought this to be a very large number but was reliably informed that this was par for the course. This was due to the very large numbers of wild animals roaming the camp.

My share of that first days hunting was a leg of chevreuil that was probably the best joint of meat I have ever tasted. It was quite clear why the hunting of boar and deer remains a big thing in France. Even more so when I noticed in the supermarket how incredibly expensive these joints of meat actually are.

If these ordinary folks were not hunting these animals themselves for meat, there is no way any of them could have afforded to buy it.

I was often asked by non-hunting folks if the hunt was dangerous and to be honest, I didn't really think so. In all my years of hunting I personally only experienced four incidents. The first was the Jean-Pierre disaster, second was perhaps the most dangerous.

I was standing at my mirador when a loud 'whis..Whis..WHIS..' noise passed inches in front of my face. It would appear that someone had spun round and shot a bullet too far out of his zone. It shot right along the line of stationary hunters finally embedding itself in a tree!

The third came when unfortunately, someone did not follow the rule of identification and had shot and killed one of the hunt dogs. He paid a big fine, bought a new dog for the owner and lost his licence.

The last happened when we were all walking back to the parked cars near the miradors. It was at the end of a hunt, so everyone was chatting about what they had seen, or more probably what they said they had seen. As we neared the cars, we discovered a nice bullet hole in somebody's car front door. He wasn't very happy!

CHAPTER NINE

The Fête Gets Organised by a Crow

Time was quickly moving on and we were approaching the traditional month when the Loser 'fête' should be held. Our successful Loto experience had provided the means to attempt the resurgence of a fête in the village. However, it did not provide enough to pay for everything, we would need to sell tickets for the meal to cover all the costs.

All we needed was a plan. Now, as an ex amateur deep-sea diver I always liked to follow the maxim 'plan the dive then dive the plan'. In other words, get a good plan together then stick to it; but this is France.

For a good start Louis, our valiant Comité chairman, was slightly injured thus not in a great mood. While cutting branches off some trees in his garden with a chainsaw, he had slipped, fallen and injured his leg. When I say fallen, I mean fallen a considerable distance down the cliff edge that bordered his house.

Luckily, he had landed on a ledge about 15 metres down and even luckier the chainsaw had landed somewhere else. However, there he was stuck and injured and waiting for the 'pompiers' to come to his rescue. Now, this was France at lunchtime, and apparently the 'pompier' team who were trained in climbing were hard to get hold of. Therefore, Louis was waiting on his ledge for a considerable time, in fact a very considerable time.

Now, don't get me wrong here as it has absolutely nothing to do with this delay, but Louis was one of the village folks who didn't like to buy the 'pompier' calendar. In fact, I am certain that this had nothing to do with any delays as there was, without any doubt, a good reason for the time lapse in their arrival.

However, I did raise my donation to 10 euros for future 'pompier' calendars just because the of the amazing good work that they do!

So, limping and not very happy Louis called a meeting of the fête Comité to plan our next move.

"So, this is all new to us," we said, "what do we actually need?"

"Well, a marquee, a dance floor, a disco, a beer tent, a dance band, someone to cook the fête meal, then stuff to do like a Vide-Grenier and a pétanque competition," Louis reeled off without breathing.

"That seems a lot for a fête," we replied, "just how long does this event actually last?"

"Two days," he said, "It has to last two days."

"Why has it got to last two days?" we questioned, already knowing what the answer was going to be.

"Because it always lasts for two days," he kindly confirmed!

There was no point in questioning this any further as everyone else was nodding in full agreement.

"So how much will all this cost?" we politely continued, again guessing the obvious answer.

"More than we have got," he confirmed for the second time.

Now at this stage we did try to convert this event into a 'what we can actually afford' type of scenario; but they wouldn't have it. The Loser fête had to last two days and contain at a minimum the aforementioned list.

"So, how are we going to pay for all this?" came our next obvious question....dreading the next answer.

"Simple, we don't pay for the band till the night, plus we only pay a deposit for the marquee, dance floor and beer tent," he happily explained.

"So, what happens if we don't sell enough tickets or it rains, and nobody turns up?" we explored.

Louis went on to defend his plan by suggesting that this could not happen as it had never happened before. He could not understand our logic that previous Comités had always had enough money to pay for everything; our Comité of course didn't. Therefore, if it all went pear shaped, we were in trouble.

We were still not convinced that firstly, we had enough activity to fill two days; and more importantly there were enough folks in the village to pay sufficient money to cover the cost. So, we suggested a few amendments.

"Why don't we cook the meal ourselves?" we offered, "something simple, and why not involve folks from a neighbouring village to boost the numbers?" And as we were warming to the theme we added "Plus, there must be a band that will do a disco as well!"

As numbers seemed to be the biggest danger, they quickly warmed to the idea of involving folks from outside the village. But in usual French style they could not envisage how this could be accomplished. It seemed a bit obvious to us, so we ploughed on.

"How about we challenge our neighbouring village to a games afternoon followed by the fête meal?" we offered. "Two village teams competing against each other with some fun events will draw in families from the other village," we explained.

Now this is where coming from village fetes in the UK pays dividends. Their obvious request as to what type of games was countered by a list of recognisable standard daft UK village fete games that you see all the time.

"Well there's welly-wanging, tug of war, slippery pole, egg and spoon race and even a wheelbarrow race," we listed, expecting some recognition.

This was met by completely blank looks followed by, "what's welly-wanging?"

We explained the concept of standing on a line to see who could lob a wellington boot the furthest. I tried desperately to avoid any questions relating to the name Wellington as the

Mayor was already a bit touchy about Waterloo. So, I continued with an enthusiastic "It's good fun, quite hard and makes great viewing for the spectators." I also added that "all these events were very easy to put on, simple to score and will be fun for everyone involved."

This was all met again by completely blank looks, but as the bar had worked and the Loto had worked they were willing to give it a try.

Jobs were quickly handed out. The complicated arrangements of the pétanque competition and Vide-Grenier were given to the mayor. These would run like clockwork, he also offered to be the judge for all the games events. We carefully suggested that the opposing Mayor ought to be involved as well, and he reluctantly agreed.

We would organise the inter-village games competition after a challenge had been accepted, again a job for the two Mayors to sort out. Louis would organise the marquee, dance floor, beer tent and band as all these were simple phone calls. Even with a dodgy leg he couldn't go wrong. And everyone would muck in with the food and cooking of the meal. It was all looking good...what could possibly go wrong?

Just to add some icing on the cake, a couple in the village actually had some guests from

America staying during the week of the fête. And, wait for it, the American guy was a chef!

"Really, I said, "er! can you ask him if he could help cook the village fête meal?"

"Yes," came the helpful reply, "I'm sure he would be thrilled."

"Best not mention the potential numbers," I continued, "or the characters he will be cooking for; or the tiny cooking facilities; or even the fact that he will be the only guy out of all the helpers who has cooked for more than 8 people!" I finished my potential pitfalls with "and don't mention that when we say help cook the meal, we actually mean, cook the meal!"

This was met by a worried 'now having second thoughts' look. However, they did ask, and the American chef was thrilled; of course he would help cook the meal. Poor guy, he had no idea what he was letting himself in for.

As for the food we kept it simple, someone knew where we could buy chicken quarters in bulk, Henri knew where he could source a large quantity of vegetables, the Professor had a friend who grew melons that would go well with ham, so that was the starter.

And finally, we went for cheese from the cheese man *(that is if we could prise him apart from the bread lady for the afternoon)* and a simple gateau for dessert. All we needed now was to know the actual numbers and that was more complex than I thought.

"When we put out the promotional material we simply give a phone number so that folks can book a seat for the meal or a table for the Vide-Grenier," we explained.

"What promotional material?" again came the universal reply, "we don't need it as everyone will know there is a fête that weekend in Loser."

"Okay, then how do people know that there happens to be a pétanque competition with prizes, a Vide-Grenier for both selling and buying, a fun games competition to watch, a band to dance to and a meal that must be booked?" we asked.

This was met by a few Gallic shrugs, some slow nodding of acknowledgement and a sudden general understanding that it pays to advertise. We quickly arranged for some posters and lots of handbills to be printed. These would be distributed to every house in the two villages, posted up in all the surrounding villages and stuck under windscreens at markets leading up to the event.

We were also concerned that sellers at the Vide-Grenier would need to be notified via the usual add in a newspaper or by attacking other Vide-Greniers with handbills before our fête. However, they all thought that this was unnecessary as "everyone will know!" So, we let it ride....unfortunately.

It was while discussing this promotional material that a thought suddenly struck me, 'book a seat for the meal'. What seat? We need seating for a couple of hundred people, and we had none whatsoever.

This was no problem apparently, as Loser always borrowed the tables and bench seating from our neighbouring village. So here we were, everything agreed and at that moment there was nothing for people to sit on!

We were lucky, our neighbours were not using their own fête seating on that weekend and were happy for us to collect and use them. And even better, Jean-Pierre volunteered to collect them with his aging tractor and trailer. This would be interesting as his trailer looked as though it was falling to bits, and the tractor didn't look capable of more than 5 or 6 MPH. We would have to do this days before the event just to get the seating back to the village.

Just to complicate matters even more, the Mayor came up with a 'great' idea for the games. He would prepare a general knowledge quiz. Now, knowing the Mayor as we did it was obvious that the questions would be along the lines "How many battles did Napoleon fight?" However, how could we say no? Thus, we agreed. *(60 by the way.)*

With everything bookable booked, apparently; and all the plans in place, probably; a group of us set off in Jean-Pierre's trailer to collect the tables and seating. I casually asked if there would be room for everyone in the trailer coming back.

To this simple request I received a few 'zuts,' a shake of heads and lots of 'bien sûr' *(of course)*. I should have known, although they had done this before it wasn't a French strike action, so it could go badly wrong.

We arrived well shaken, covered in dust and smelling of the diesel which seemed to seep out of every joint in Jean-Pierre's tractor. Also, the strange sheep smell from the trailer now seemed to have transferred itself to all its passengers.

The tables and bench seating were piled up under a huge tarpaulin, and when revealed they were somewhat disappointing. Not the new shiny tables and benches that were described in glowing terms to me. These were the rejects that the other village had just replaced!

However, any port in a storm so we started to pile them into the trailer. Now it was quickly becoming clear that we would need all these tables and the pile was getting dangerously high. My suggestion for two trips was quickly discounted as unnecessary and on they went piling them up.

It was now beginning to look like a giant game of Jenga but at least we were finally done, and Jean-Pierre was securing everything in place with string.

Yes, you did read that correctly, with bits of blue string. I have never worked out the reasoning behind the blue string that French farmers use to block off a path, divert cows away from a road or even use as a no-entry signal. But you see it everywhere you go.

You can just picture the scene as two marauding bandits creep up to your house to rob it one night. There across the entrance is a piece of blue string; completely foiled they head off back home!

Having completed his task to everyone's satisfaction, except me, Jean-Pierre jumped in the cab of the tractor and the band of willing volunteers started to climb on top of the pile of tables and bench seats. I was manhandled up last, still questioning the 'Health and Safety' aspects of their construction; and, off we went.

At every bend in the road, at every bump and at every slight gradient, the stack of tables and seats seemed to move as though they had a life of their own. Meanwhile the happy band of helpers were hanging desperately to the top of the pile. To anyone driving in the opposite direction it must have looked like a scene from the old TV gameshow Jeux Sans Frontières, you could almost hear the commentator Stuart Hall crying with laughter at every turn.

Somehow, we arrived in the village square in one piece just as another French 'Health and Safety' example was being played out by Marcel and Maurice. They had volunteered to put up the fête lights across the square. However, these lights had not been used for years, due to the challenging fiscal ideas of the previous Comité, therefore were suspect.

Now, having untangled the tens of metres of lighting, which probably took some considerable time, they were dangling them across the square. This was by means of Marcel slowly moving the village tractor with Maurice precariously balanced high up in the raiseable huge metal bucket attached to the front.

The plan being for Maurice to play out the lights as Marcel's tractor slowly moved. I did not have the heart to ask if they had checked the lights before doing this....as we were about to find out; obviously not.

Their progress was being somewhat hampered by the village crow. This huge black bird kept sitting on the lights near Maurice's head squawking out its own instructions. And Maurice nearly toppled over each time he took a swipe at it.

The bird belonged to the 'infirmière' *(nurse)* who lived in the village, it was his pet and mostly lived in an enclosure on his terrace. However, often it would get out and cause havoc chewing the mastic out of people's window frames, eating expensive pool covers, divebombing cats and dogs and generally causing mayhem.

The lights were finally connected to various plug points on people's terraces at each side of the square; without asking permission of course. And with Maurice finally descending it was time to switch on and take in the stunning visual effect.

Nothing; nothing happened, it was a bit like that game you play each year with your Christmas tree lighting but on a much grander scale. This was accompanied by several squawks from the crow that sounded too much like laughter.

So, up went Maurice again, this time to dangle dangerously over the side of the bucket at each bulb to give it a poke. Each movement of the swaying bucket resulted in loud 'putains' from Maurice and many 'zuts' from Marcel. At least he managed this task without saying 'fuck off' every 5 minutes!

Meanwhile, we were in the line of fire underneath this activity unloading our game of Jenga. It was quite clear that these tables and benches would all need washing, repairing and a bit of sanding else most of the fête guests would be going home with splinters where they least needed them! So much for neighbouring village generosity.

Ian, another Brit, who lived in the square had been woken up by someone dangling on a tractor bucket in front of his terrace windows. Unfazed by the fact that his terrace now had strings of lights attached to it, he had wandered down to help. He made rather nice items out of wood, anything from doors, gates to wine racks etc. All to a high quality, so his look of dismay at our pile of potential wooden tables and benches spoke volumes.

"Are you sure about this?" he asked.

"Sure, they will be fine," I answered

His look made it clear that we had a bit of a challenge. When someone who actually makes things from wood thinks that we might not be able to turn these old tables into....well...tables, you know you are in trouble.

Just at that moment the marquee lorry arrived at the same time as the beer tent van. Things were getting a bit busy.

Now here's a thing; if you ordered a huge marquee for your village square wouldn't you, at the very least, measure out the square to judge what size was needed? Well Louis had either overlooked this minor task or had just gone for 'a big one please'.

As the construction guys that delivered the marquee started its erection, it was becoming clear that it would take up almost all of the square, block off two of the entrances and probably limit almost everything else we had planned. For a start the pétanque competition, that I was reliably informed always took place in the square and its surrounding roads, would now go in, out and around a huge marquee.

This wouldn't be so much of a problem except that inside the marquee a stage was being set up for the band and a wooden dance floor. This wooden dance floor was expensive to hire, much like the marquee, and therefore was questioned as to how necessary it actually was.

Again, I was hit by, "they always have a wooden dance floor." Why they couldn't just dance on the road surface was beyond me. It was also becoming clear that huge as it was, there was not enough room for all the tables and seating to go inside the marquee.

"So where do you put all the tables and seating?" I casually enquired.

"Next to the marquee," came the response.

"Okay, so what if it rains?" I countered.

This produced blank looks all round as they waited for each other to answer. An almost universal "It never rains," completed the debate!

At this point, with the marquee guys hammering huge metal pegs into the tarmac road, everyone was making their way over to the beer tent. Now, by beer tent what I actually mean is a large number of, what looked like, scaffolding poles. These were next to a pile of various sized tarpaulins which hopefully made up the roof and sides. So, this was not a beer tent, it was an Ikea type do-it-yourself challenge.

I rather stupidly asked where the assembly instructions were, this was greeted by "it's easy, we have done this loads of times." And off they went. As to the age-old conundrum of 'how many Frenchmen does it take to erect a beer tent?' well in this case about 12!

Poles were being picked up then put down, they were being laid in the road to judge sizes by one person and, while their back was turned, picked up by someone else. Tarpaulin was being held up to the light as if this would explain its actual usage, meanwhile the beer tent guys were unloading large metal kegs of beer with the beer tap equipment. Again, no instructions, and with a quick 'bonne chance' *(good luck)* they were gone.

So just to recap, we had a half erected huge marquee taking up most of the village square. We had massive metal marquee pegs being hammered into the tarmac of the road. We had strings of ancient lights hanging dangerously low across the square that, as yet, didn't work. And we had a pile of poles, tarpaulin and beer kegs that constituted the fête beer tent. Plus, a lot of very puzzled looks and a crow.

At this point Maurice, who maintained that he knew all about erecting beer tents, took command of the poles. This was clearly just to get him away from the dodgy lights problem.

But luckily Bernard, our professional do-everything guy, had turned up and tackled the lights. So, for us it was back to pole by pole assembly of the beer tent.

Now, what we did know was that the beer tent was meant to be square, at least that gave us a fighting chance. So, with one group assembling the roof and others putting together the walls we were getting there.

Finally, we had some sort of structure together and on went the tarpaulin roof and the sides that fitted underneath the beer tent serving bar. This wooden bar went completely around the four walls leaving just a gap for entry and exit. Sweating and dirty from the task at hand we all stepped back to admire our work. It had taken about an hour and a half.

Then it suddenly dawned on me, dare I mention it? I had to mention it, could I just wait a bit and let someone else mention it?

"Er! shouldn't the bar be on the inside?" I asked, while trying to pretend that this minor point wouldn't matter.

"Putain!" said Maurice.

"Merde alors!" completed everyone else.

And off they went again, the whole thing was taken to bits and rebuilt. This time with the bar on the inside, meanwhile the crow sat on one of the beer kegs slowly shaking its head from side to side.

After 45 minutes we were done, and it actually looked like a beer tent. The Professor was already busy inside setting up the taps for the metal beer kegs. He must have known what he was doing because within minutes he was filling plastic beer glasses for us to test its worthiness.

Never has a glass of beer tasted so good, either that or we were all dying of thirst! Just at that moment the lights lit up amongst much cheering and Bernard gave an overly dramatic bow from the tractor bucket. Even the crow looked happy.

Leaving a group of folks trying to tidy up the tables and chairs I wandered over to the village hall to check on the progress of everything else. Louis was there holding court and discussing the games for the village challenge.

Outside the hall we had arranged for a rectangle of straw bales, donated from our favourite shepherd, to be laid on the floor. Over this was placed a huge agriculture black plastic cover. Into the cover a large hose was pouring water at a vast rate slowly making a makeshift shallow swimming pool.

Next to the pool was a long wooden pole which would be laid across the pool to make our 'slippery pole' game. For some reason the pole looked suspiciously like the old telegraph pole that had gone missing from the front of Jean-Pierre's farmhouse! I had located a rope for the tug of war and some redundant wellington boots for the welly-wanging, so all was coming together.

However, there was clearly a bit of tension between Louis and the Mayor as they discussed the general knowledge quiz. Apparently, Louis felt that no one would know any of the answers, but the Mayor insisted that they would. I couldn't comment as I didn't understand the questions anyway thus simply gave a shrug and left them to it.

Suddenly I was confronted by several huge rusty metal containers covered in a rusty metal grill. The last time I had seen these they were at the army camp and were used, apparently, for the soldiers to make a massive bar-b-que.

"Er! what are these for?" I shouted to Louis.

"To cook the chicken," he responded.

I should have guessed of course; how else could you possibly cook 200 chicken quarters? I just hoped it would be too dark for anyone to see what a state the cooking implements were in. At that moment Ollie pulled up in his car back from his quest to purchase knives, forks and spoons.

We had previously agreed that we should use some of the Loto money to buy enough cutlery for about 200 people as this would cost-in over the years and they would be used many, many times.

"Good news," he said, "I've managed to pick up a bargain."

"Great," I replied, genuinely pleased that something had gone to plan.

At this Ollie retrieved a large box of silver coloured 'plastic' knives, forks and spoons from the boot of his car.

"But we wanted metal cutlery," I pointed out, "eating with plastic knives and forks is a nightmare."

"Ah! but don't you see?" he said, "these are silver coloured and look like metal!"

By now I was beginning to lose the will to live so let it go, and anyway, what was that big pile of tins doing in the corner of the hall?

"What are these?" I again interrupted Louis.

"That's the vegetables for the meal," he responded.

So, Henri, you know, the guy that grows massive amounts of his own fruit and vegetables, and had volunteered to source the vegetables for the village meal; had delivered a large quantity of huge catering tins of veg! I was a bit dumfounded by this turn of events and began to wonder what our American chef was going to make of it all. I wouldn't be surprised if he did a runner.

With just a couple of days to go it was time for a meeting of the Comité to see how everything was going. So far, we had our 'chapiteau' *(our marquee)* including stage and dance floor, our beer tent, the tables and chairs, cutlery *(thanks Ollie)*, some lights, all the accoutrements for the games and a chef. We also had a team of volunteers for the games challenge match.

In the corner of the hall were stacked a large quantity of huge tins of veg, the fridge was packed with chicken and Parma ham, and in another corner a huge pile of melons were waiting to be cut up.

In fact, there were at least twice as many melons as actually needed because the Professor had forgotten that melons are cut in half for the starter course. And finally, large quantities of booze lay everywhere ready for the off.

"So how are the ticket sales going Louis?" I asked.

"Great," he replied, "we have almost sold all 200 tickets meal tickets."

That was good news, so I explored a bit further, "how many have actually paid?"

"None," he said, "I told them to pay on the day."

This was worrying, what if they didn't turn up?

"How many Vide-Grenier tables are we expecting?" I continued.

"Don't know," he said, "we will not know until the day."

So, we had advertised a Vide-Grenier and didn't even know if there would be any tables selling stuff. In fact, there seemed to be an awful lot of 'don't knows' for this stage of the game and my question about the number of pétanque competitors met with the same answer.

With a somewhat sinking feeling I turned to count tins of veg and noticed that the chef had just arrived. With my best smiley face, I thanked him for his help and showed him around.

"So, how many are we cooking for?" came his first obvious question, all the time looking with some distain at the smallish cooker in the village hall kitchen.

"Er! about 200 people," I replied, whilst trying to sound as though this was absolutely no problem.

"Okay, so where is the kitchen?" he asked, while looking with great suspicion at the pile of tinned veg.

"This is it," I responded, quickly adding "but we have a large bar-b-que outside."

"Okay, so what is the menu?" he continued, all the time looking round to check that there was no 'Game for a Laugh' television camera hidden somewhere.

I went on to explain our simple melon with Parma ham, chicken with vegetables, cheese and finally gateaux. So basically, here we had a professional chef who had been hoodwinked into cooking for 200 French folks with tins of veg! He shook his head, looked sadly around, thought about it for a moment; a moment that seemed to last about 30 minutes to us, and then said "Okay, let's do it."

It's not the first time that America has come to the aid of a French catastrophe and it probably won't be the last, but at least we now had a fighting chance with the meal. Just at that moment as I was feeling a bit relieved, Ollie popped his head round the door.

"They're practicing," he said.

"Who's practicing?" we all replied in unison.

"The other village team, they're out practicing the games, at the moment they're lobbing wellies,"

Now here was something that I had not even thought of, the other village really wanted to win the challenge and we had no time to get our team together to do likewise. However, thinking about the size of some of our team, I couldn't see them losing the tug of war nor the wellie-wanging, so just gave a very French 'je m'en fous', in this case meaning 'whatever!'

As I turned back, I could see that our chef had opened a large tin of French beans and had pulled out a very sad looking example for perusal. He looked at me with a 'you have to be kidding' look!

Chapter Ten

The Big Day Amid Welly Mayhem

It was a bright, clear and sunny day as I set off for the short walk into the centre of the village. As I passed Bernard's house, he was in the garden again taking a piss and he waved a jolly 'bonjour' as I passed by.

Each time I passed by his house I always wondered at the strange extension that he had built at the rear of his property. Here was a shining example of how to put people off from using you for any type of work. It looked as though a child had constructed a giant Lego building and attached it to an old farmhouse.

How he ever had been granted planning permission for this 'construction' I will never know. Actually, I did know, he never asked for it; and nobody seemed to care. It was a lesson I learned over the years in France, stop worrying about changing number plates on your UK car, getting a French driving licence, registering your

UK caravan for its French number..etc. etc. Nobody cares much anyway.

It was the first day of our fête and I could already hear music coming from the square. And when I arrived, I was somewhat shocked to see that the beer tent was already in big demand with the Professor valiantly manning the bar.

Unfortunately, he was also in charge of the huge coffee urn which was already switched on and stewing. We had bought some red tee shirts for our inter-village challenge team and they seemed well pleased as we handed them out.

Maurice was fiddling with something on the steps of the Mairie and my sense of 'it's all going well' disappeared as I noticed that he was setting up the chasse sound system for the Mayor. This, apparently, was for him to make his welcoming speeches; and would also be used for his general knowledge quiz. What could possibly go wrong?

With the second day of the fête to be all about the Vide-Grenier, the pétanque competition and a disco; today was dedicated to the inter-village games. Interspersed, of course, with music, dancing and the evening event, the fête meal. In fact, our chef was already in the village hall planning out his day and giving instructions by hand signals to the volunteers willing to lend a hand.

He had been out since early in the morning buying herbs and spices that he would use, apparently, to make the tinned vegetables taste like...well, vegetables. Good luck with that one. He also had a plan to overcome the large number of people who would need serving chicken all at the same time.

His plan here was to part cook half of the chicken quarters in various ovens. These would be placed on the bar-b-que to quickly finish off and served first. At the same time the other half of the uncooked chicken quarters would be completely cooked on the bar-b-que to be served last. Well, that was the plan anyway!

Large numbers of people were beginning to mill about, and our opposing team had arrived thus it was down to the Mayor to welcome everyone and start the proceedings. This was somewhat hampered by our crow who had found it amusing to divebomb people who were wearing hats. Everyone seemed to ignore this as though it was a normal occurrence, perhaps it was!

About every third word of the opening speech was being missed due to the erratic functioning of the sound system, however it looked like everyone understood what he was saying. And with that, everyone lined up to watch the games. The first was the tug-of-war; and it was.....war. We had insisted that the opposing teams would have both male and female team members for every game. So, it was a bit disheartening to see that our female tug-of-war opponents were larger than our male team members.

And with a signal from the Mayor they were off. Much shouting, swearing, name calling and micky taking drowned out the music still coming from the marquee, and that was just from the children! The crow was also becoming very excited, as he sat on the lights strung across the square squawking his encouragement to the home team.

With one pull won by each team it came down to the last tug to decide the winner, and this went on for some time. Both sides straining and grunting as they battled for the win. I thought of perhaps mentioning that it was only a game; but to these folks it clearly was not, so on it went. Finally, someone slipped on the home team, they fell over and lost it.

You would have thought that the winning team had just won the Olympics not a tug-of-war. By the same token it looked like the losing team had just been told that they were being shot at dawn. This was all a bit serious, not the fun games we had in mind.

Luckily the next two events were calmer in nature, an egg and spoon race round a straw bale assault course and a wheel barrow race. By now it was lunchtime, and everyone was crowding around the beer tent where baguettes and cheese were disappearing fast and kegs of beer were emptying.

Some of the potential beer customers were being put off by our crow who, seeing the bread, was now sat on the bar squawking his demands for lunch. It was pointless pushing him away as he just came back again.

As is usual in France this lunchbreak lasted for several hours during which time there seemed to be a growing interest in the welly-wanging implements that I had left by the road. This was further prompted by the Mayor, who was pacing out and marking each metre distance along the road alongside the Mairie. For some unknown reason he had anticipated that the throwers would all manage to throw the wellington in the desired direction; as it turned out this was a bit optimistic.

There were several disadvantages to the Mayor's choice of welly-wanging venue. Firstly, there were cars parked along the chosen road. Secondly, the fête lights hung dangerously close overhead. Thirdly, there happened to be houses along this road which just happened to have windows. And lastly nobody had put up a sign at the other end of the road to announce possible flying wellington boots. Thus, any incoming traffic was in danger of being bombarded!

With all this in mind I watched as the two teams lined up for the start of the match. I decided to give a quick demonstration on how to effectively throw a welly, unfortunately it turned out to be a demonstration on how not to throw a welly; never mind. I had a funny feeling about this event, somehow throwing a wellington boot in the middle of a field in the UK had felt safe. Here it felt like an oncoming disaster.

The first guy to throw managed to hit the lights which spun the boot round causing the crow to squawk in terror and fly off back to the beer tent. After two spins round the lighting it dropped about 50 cm from his feet. Some ironic 'bravos' were not accepted gladly by the thrower who stormed off.

Next to stand up was Jean-Pierre, why he was picked I will never know. I would have thought that a better choice would have been Madam Vay, she would probably have thrown the welly into the next village. Still no sign of her husband!

After much spinning of the welly, in a circle above his head, he let go. It went flying backwards bouncing off a lamppost landing nicely on the roof of the beer tent. The crow had now worked out that this was all a personal attack on him, and was getting a bit agitated. Further attempts at throwing were causing mayhem. Bouncing off car roofs, stuck in trees, hitting windows, nearly decapitating spectators and sometimes even landing in the actual road.

However, each time the Mayor treated the throw to a great deal of technical measurement and a careful logging in his book. Did these villagers realise that their attempts at lobbing a wellington boot were being professionally recorded by the Mayor? And would probably be logged somewhere in the Mairie's massive archives for future generation to laugh at?

A car that innocently turned the corner and drove into this sporting scenario was shouted at, booed and severely castigated as though the poor driver had purposely tried to sabotage some global contest. He slowly drove through the crowd looking shame faced only to find that the only way to escape was by driving through the marquee! Suddenly by some fluke one of our team let loose a mighty throw that sent the boot to the other end of the road, and the event was over.

I had time to check out the progress of the meal and dashed back to the village hall as the Mayor was preparing for his general knowledge quiz. The chef looked about ten years older, was red in the face, had beads of perspiration and was shaking his head as he tasted a trial run of cooked tin vegetables.

"Do they actually eat this stuff here?" he enquired.

"Of course, they love it," I helpfully lied. What I didn't add was the fact that they would all be a bit tipsy by then, so it didn't really matter. I also felt that mentioning this fact would not help boost his ego as a professional chef.

With a whining feedback noise coming from the now recognisable chasse sound system I headed back to the start of the general knowledge quiz. As I passed by the beer tent someone was spitting out the contents of his coffee cup onto the floor while making choking noises. So, the Professor's coffee was going down well then! Meanwhile another beer tent attendee was wrestling with the crow to get his baguette lunch back!

The two teams stood politely as the Mayor read out each question in turn. The plan was that the first team member to answer each question correctly scored a point. However, so far just blank looks, a few shaking of heads and some murmurings of some of the words that you met in chapter 5 were all that were forthcoming. It was quite clear that the Mayor's 'general knowledge' quiz was more like a 'not general knowledge' quiz.

Luckily among his list of questions he had included a few that he had thought easy, obvious or almost childlike. And these were quickly answered at least making it look as though the teams were scoring points.

(We had all this again years later when the Mayor insisted that a walk around the village answering questions related to the history of Loser would be a great idea. We saw his questions before the event; and after translating them, I hit google to come up with the answers.

I couldn't answer one of them or should I say google couldn't answer one of them. On testing a few questions with an elderly member of the village, whose family had lived in Loser for generations, it became clear that nobody would ever know the answers.

Luckily on the actual day it was blisteringly hot and not one person signed up for the walk. Unfortunately, the Mayor simply said, "no problem, I will save them for another year!")

The band had now arrived and were setting up in the marquee, I think aging hippies is the best description. However, apparently, they had a big

287

following as the local village folk love their traditional dancing music. This was good news for us as they would attract in potential customers for the beer tent.

Meanwhile our helpers were covering the aging tables with paper to hide their rather sad condition and plastic knives, forks and spoons were being positioned. I must admit, that from 30 metres they actually looked like metal ones.

Just to add to the ambiance, red wine had been poured from the local supermarket's large 5L carton containers into emptied plastic water bottles. Not all the same of course, the empty bottles had been collected for weeks by anyone who had drunk some mineral water. Therefore, all manufacturer's sizes, shapes and colours were represented!

These were distributed along the line of tables and were complimented by plastic drinking glasses. So, for all you environment friendly non-plastic advocates, this would have been the meal from hell. Just to be clever I had made up a 'special' plastic bottle of wine and left it by our seat positions.

Next to arrive was what looked like hundreds of baguettes. Knowing what food was about to be served up, I guessed that these would be quite popular!

So back again to the big contest, with the score as a tie between the two competing teams, it was everyone to the slippery pole event. Now, as we had described it, this contest was all about one team after another trying to cross a wet pole. They would all have to try and achieve this, from one end to the other, without falling in the pool.

However, this is France, and nothing is allowed to be that easy. Unbeknown to us, Louis had squirted washing-up liquid along the pole and armed one of the teams with a large number of plastic balls. With these they were to bombard their competitors; supposedly as the team members attempted each crossing.

You can imagine the scene, unless you are from the Health and Safety Department in which case try not to imagine the scene. As each team member tried to slowly slip along the very slippery pole, they were immediately bombarded by a large number of plastic balls hitting them at a frightening velocity. And no account was taken for ladies or children, they were all blasted at the same rate.

Very soon the balls were being thrown at any member of the opposing team, even those standing well away from the slippery pole. Meanwhile the water in the pool was becoming covered in suds and large bubbles from the ever-increasing amount of washing-up liquid that was slipping in off people's feet. And, of course, after the continual replenishment from Louis's supply.

As a background to this mayhem a smoky cloud had descended on the spectators from the now roaring bar-b-que that Maurice had helped along by kindly adding some White Spirit!

Through the smoke, Madam Vay could be seen staring at me, struggling to put a name to my face. Thank God that I was not wearing my leather coat. Now all hell had let loose round the very, very slippery pole as people were being thrown into the pool, balls were bouncing off anyone's head, Louis was running up and down waving his arms about trying to calm everything down; and a soaked Mayor was stood there heroically trying to keep score on his soapy notebook.

A rather frazzled chef with a smoke blackened face saved the day by announcing that the fête meal was ready. And the Mayor helped close the event down by shouting that it was an honourable draw. It was quite a sight to see the two village Mayors shake hands, soaked to the skin and covered with soap suds!

Therefore, with the band playing in the background, and sodden folk returning from the slippery pole, it was time to serve up the food.

Most of the conversation was about the baffling general knowledge quiz, and with their soapy puzzled looks, we started the meal.

It is surprising how fast you can get 200 people to sit down when there is already wine on the table. The poor Professor was quickly left all on his own at the beer tent with his new-found mate, the crow!

As they all tucked in to their melon starter, Henri had wandered over to the bar-b-que to peruse the cooking chicken. Now he was not party to the chef's plans of pre-cooking, so simply thought he could help matters along by swapping the chicken around the top of the bar-b-que. This being done to share out the hottest parts of the grill while turning most of the chicken quarters over.

Now this had the unforeseen, unfortunate consequence of mixing up the part-cooked chicken with the uncooked chicken. And with this kindly service complete and his hands casually clasped behind his back, Henri wandered over to his melon.

Ollie meanwhile was busy selling tombola tickets. He and Louis had been impressed with the Loto tombola success thus were easily persuaded to try again. He seemed to be having a similar result, probably spurred on by the less than sober state of most of the diners. I asked Louis when he would do the draw for the winner and he confirmed that during the evenings dance would be a good idea.

People were lining up now for the main course and the chef was serving chicken, having carefully taken his pre-cooked chicken quarters from the bar-b-que first. The queue was moving slowly as most folk were standing staring at the vegetables to try and guess as to what they actually were.

I allayed their doubts by suggesting that these vegetables had been cooked in a traditional American method. They seemed happy with this and like all French folk they simply accepted that nobody, outside of France, could really cook anything. This was quickly confirmed by the first then second plates returning with undercooked chicken.

Henri's helping chicken 'shuffle' had mixed up the chef's carefully pre-cooked chicken with the uncooked chicken with their position on the bar-b-que. Thus, when the chef had removed half of the chicken quarters knowing them to be thoroughly cooked....they were not! He was horrified, how could this happen? Here was a professional chef being forced to dish out unrecognisable canned vegetables accompanied by blackened undercooked chicken. He was mortified.

Chicken quarters were cut through to reveal that at least half on display were not cooked, meanwhile those that had been pre-cooked were becoming nicely overcooked. This was not looking good and our valiant chef was now running between the bar-b-que and the serving tables trying to put things right.

To give our unfortunate diners their due nobody seemed to complain and just poured another glass of wine; while struggling with bendy knives and forks. Most of the guys had given up completely with the plastic and had reverted to pocket knives and fingers!

Jean-Pierre, in particular, could be seen happily munching on an obviously raw piece of chicken completely oblivious to anything. It was then that I noticed that my nicely aged, decanted Chateauneuf du Pape was missing.

I had decanted a nice bottle into a plastic water bottle and had placed it in front of our seating for the meal. Jean-Pierre and Madeline had reached across the table and 'borrowed' it and were busily emptying the contents; leaving me with a nice bottle of supermarket special. At least it wasn't one of his vintages....I hoped.

So, with the questionable chicken now being digested and the cheese and gateau now consumed, the music was getting louder. The fête lights were beginning to flicker from welly damage as Louis tried to announce the start of the dancing in the marquee. Again, the chasse sound system cut out every third word, but folks got the general idea and started to wander away from the dining tables.

The Professor was back in business at the beer tent, but the crow had disappeared. Someone had seen him drinking from a glass of Ricard and he wasn't seen again for several days!

It had been a long interesting day, so we left the party early to catch up on some sleep as the Vide-Grenier would start very early the next morning. As I glanced back, I could see our chef sat shaking his head in disbelief with a very large glass of Scotch in his hand.

The villagers were dancing faster and faster as they got into the traditional dancing with increasing gusto; and for some reason a rather inebriated villager appeared to be running around scaring people dressed in a Darth Vader costume. I think now that it may have been Henri keeping a low profile!

The next day we strolled down to the village square nice and early, we were lucky as it proved to be yet another clear sunny day for the fête. We were met by a rather disconsolate Louis who was in discussion with both Maurice and Ollie.

"What's the problem?" I asked.

"It's the Vide-Grenier sellers," he replied.

"So, what has happened?" I continued, thinking that they were all fighting over the best positions.

"There isn't any!" he said, "well actually there are three."

So there we were, having posted handbills everywhere broadcasting a Vide-Grenier, only for potential buyers to turn up to find just a few tables. However, at least large numbers of pétanque players were turning up and the Mayor was already at a table in the square noting down teams.

It was an interesting, very French day with folk arriving in large numbers to peruse three Vide-Grenier tables, pétanque players lobbing heavy metal balls through the marquee and a lot of very hung-over people hanging round the beer tent; mostly drinking the Professor's stewed coffee.

We met up with the chef later in the afternoon and profusely thanked him for all his efforts. All he would say was "do not tell anyone in America that I served up tinned vegetables and raw chicken!"

I was glad when the disco was under way and the Comité had a drink to celebrate the end of a busy two days.

"The meal seemed to go okay," said Henri, while trying to look completely innocent.

"The slippery pole was a success," remarked Louis, "although I think we put too much soap in the water!"

"WE?" said everyone in unison.

"Anyway," I said, "who won the tombola in the end?"

There was a deathly quiet followed by a "merde!" from Louis. They had sold about 300 tickets and forgotten to draw the winning number!

EPILOGUE

It was yet another hot sunny day in Loser and a very sad one for us. The removal lorry had left, we had said our goodbyes, the car was full of fuel, the caravan was hitched, and our two dogs sat patiently waiting for their new adventure.

Not the two dogs we had arrived with of course, they now lay buried forever looking over the valley that had been their happy home for many years. We arrived with two happy English dogs, Fritz and Truda; and left with two equally happy French ones, Barney and Jessie.

After many years enjoying our new French life in this rather special village, we had decided that the time had come for a last adventure in a different part of France. I am not sure that our French friends in Loser could understand our decision. They all were born in the area or in Loser itself and would remain there forever. A family home to them was a true lasting commodity that passed down through the generations.

They couldn't see how everything was rapidly changing with young people quickly moving away to big towns and cities for work, and to be fair, more of an exciting life.

Unfortunately, the enthusiasm for activity in the village had once again died down with the collapse of the most recent Comité des Fêtes, and most of the items we had once purchased were now sat waiting for some new blood to take on the task again.

As I was about to climb into the car, I could hear that now recognisable foot trundling sound, along with the distinctive smell of sheep. And along the road came Jean-Pierre. Behind him came his new collie dog trotting along tied to a piece of string. His faithful old collie had finally had enough and just laid down and died. The sheep would have to get along without him.

"Salut Jean-Pierre," I said, "fait beau."

"Grrahe mer mer mergrr gru," he replied.

"Oui, bien sûr," I said, "mer grr gru grunbrr."

We both laughed, he waved, and wandered off to tend his sheep for yet another exciting day. Shortly after leaving Loser we heard that Jean-Pierre's sister had put his farm up for sale. After his mother's death the farm was owned by them both and she now wanted it gone, leaving just the family house for Jean-Pierre and Madeline.

He was well into his seventies now and long overdue for retirement. So, probably one of the last real shepherds had hung up his battered hat. And with that, his method of tending sheep had been confined to history.

He didn't go without his usual controversy though. He had an argument with the Mayor about shooting his gun very early in the morning and waking everyone up. Jean-Pierre retaliated by pulling a very old wooden hay wain with his tractor and parking it on his land opposite the Mayor's house. He then set light to it! The scorched remains being seen every day as the Mayor left his residence.

Jean-Pierre complimented this kind action by putting barbed wire round each of his fields that surrounded the Mayor's property, thus hindering any walking that the Mayor wanted to do with his dogs. The moral here was clear, don't mess with the shepherd!

The End

A note from the author:

Many thanks for reading 'French Farce', I hope that you enjoyed the book as much as I enjoyed writing it.

If you could spare the time to leave a review with Amazon I would very much appreciate it. Reviews are the lifeblood for authors and help considerably with future projects.

In fact it was the success and fantastic reviews left for my first book, 'Please Wipe Your Boots', that prompted this second foray into the travail that is writing.

Stanley George

Some Amazon reviews for 'Please Wipe Your Boots' (ISBN 978-1517584474)

The irreverent, humorous misadventures of a GPO telephone apprentice in the 60s.

"Read from cover to cover non-stop. Thoroughly enjoyable, well written and easy to follow."

"This is a must read; I fell about laughing at some of the tales. Yes, it was a different age and such antics now would be frowned upon; but we survived, and the world kept turning."

"This book is excellent and had me in tears."

"An absolutely brilliant book and a story extremely well told. I have now read the book three times."

"What a great read, it brought back many happy memories. Once started I could not put it down."

"A superb read...buy it!"

"Once I started reading it I just could not put it down. So true but now seems almost unbelievable. Great book.

About the author:

Stanley George had a very successful career in telecommunications spanning 33 years. He started this journey as a GPO telephone apprentice and finished as Head of HR for British Telecom Networks.

On retiring to a small village in the south of France he had time to reflect on the humorous adventures along the way. And this led to the writing of the memoir 'Please Wipe Your Boots'.

However, rural France uncovered much the same bizarre events and strange characters that matched the mayhem that was the GPO. Therefore 'French Farce' almost wrote itself.

Printed in Great Britain
by Amazon